Complete Embellishing

To Leah -
Happy Crafting !
♡ Kaytie

Complete Embellishing

Easy techniques and over 30 great projects

CREATIVE HOMEOWNER®

Home Arts

First published in North America in 2008 by

ISBN 10: 1-58011-401-6
ISBN 13: 978-1-58011-401-1
Library of Congress Control Number: 2007935782

Current printing (last digit)
10 9 8 7 6 5 4 3 2 1

Produced by Collins & Brown
10 Southcombe Street
London
W14 0RA

An imprint of Anova Books Company Ltd.

Commissioning Editor: Michelle Lo
Photographers: Mark Winwood and Michael Wicks
Designer: Sarah Rock
Production Controller: Morna McPherson
Technical Editor: Emily Harste

Printed and Bound in China

CREATIVE HOMEOWNER
A Division of Federal Marketing Corp.
24 Park Way
Upper Saddle River, NJ 07458

www.creativehomeowner.com

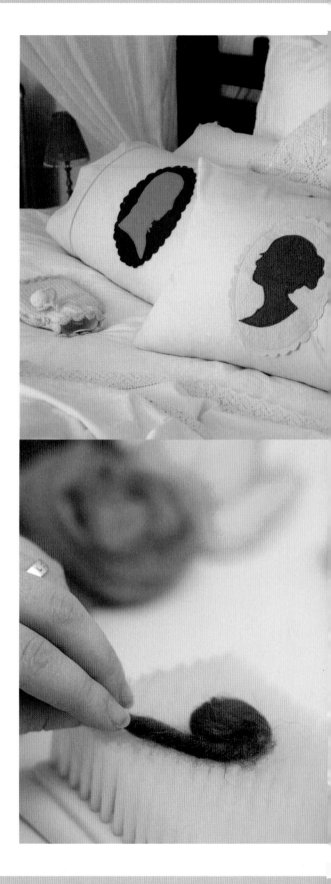

Contents

Introduction

I grew up in a crafty house. My mom was the ultimate do-it-yourself mother; our baby food was homemade; our clothes were hand-sewn; and as a child, my favorite toys were a bunch of wooden spoons, painted to resemble our family. When I wanted or needed something, my mom's first thought was not "Where do I buy it?" but "How do I make it?" Things were never thrown away; they were recycled and used for another purpose. I never really thought that I was missing anything then and now I know that I wasn't.

Don't get me wrong—I went through my rebellious phase. I practically lived at the mall in 8th grade, and all I wanted was to look like everyone else. Fitting in was paramount and my crafty upbringing was not doing me any favors. Or was it? Looking back, I see things a little differently—my family couldn't afford all the mall clothes I wanted, but thanks to my thrifty upbringing, I knew that I could find a lot of the same designer labels in secondhand shops. And all of those fancy parties my friends invited me to? My mom made my dresses and no one ever knew. Just because you're crafty doesn't mean you have to look like a home-ec project. Even if I was rejecting the DIY lifestyle on the outside, it was the only way I got through those tough middle-school years.

Flash forward quite a few years: I was living in Connecticut, working in New Jersey, and I was miserable. I hated where I lived; I hated my job; I didn't relate to any of my friends; and I had no creative energy. I sat in front of a computer all day aimlessly surfing the web, looking for something I could grasp onto. One day, I found it. I had started getting back into crafting and I spent a lot of time looking for crafty sites on the Web. Most of them were not really my style, but I would take the techniques I learned and mold them into something that I thought was cool. One fateful day, I stumbled upon getcrafty.com, and my life changed. I know what you're thinking—it's pretty sad that my life changed with a Web site right? Wrong—here was a Web site devoted to cool, feminist women making crafts and, oh wow, here was this message board full of women talking about it, talking about everything—from making skirts and canning vegetables to their jobs and their boyfriends and girlfriends, and everything in between. It was a revelation to find that there were people out there like me.

After a while, some of us decided we should meet. There were tons of ladies in New York City and I lived close enough to come in on the train. I was pleasantly surprised to find out that I liked these people offline as much as I had liked them online. Here was a strong group of women (and a few token guys) who really "got" me. I am still friends with many of these people to this day: many of us are now pursuing crafts as full-time jobs; others prefer to make things for fun; but all of us are better for our love of crafts.

In the last few years, the craft movement has

continued to grow stronger and gain more respect: craft blogs are popping up everywhere; the Museum of Art and Design in New York recently held exhibits for artists who use crochet, lace-making, and embroidery in a fine-art context; and when young tattooed hipsters on the subway pull out their knitting, no one even blinks. Once upon a time, you might tell someone at a party that you were crafty and they would imagine their grandmothers at home making crocheted tissue-box covers (not that there's anything wrong with them—I love those things!) but today people actually have a reference point for craftiness and they know the myriad forms it takes. That's pretty cool. Crafting has come out of the proverbial closet and I couldn't be happier that more and more people are picking up knitting needles and embroidery hoops to make things themselves.

There is nothing more satisfying than making something with your own two hands. Of course it's easier to buy a new sweater at the mall, but lots of people already have that sweater. I love shopping and fashion as much as the next lady (actually, no, I love it a whole lot more) but I've learned that it's much more rewarding and fun (not to mention more economical and environmentally sound) to work with what I have. When I want a new sweater or a cooler bag, I just go through my closet and try to reinvent something. Maybe that boring A-line skirt needs some ruffles or those jeans (that have been crumpled

in a ball on the floor for months) would look better as a skirt. I love all of my clothes, but I am only truly proud of the items that I have made. By the way, this feeling extends to the way I decorate my home, too. Everything I own is open to embellishing!

Of course, in all my years of crafting, there have been some disasters too. There was the time that I tried to make a knit dress from a one-way stretch fabric, and cut the fabric in the direction that doesn't stretch; or that really late night in college, when, fueled by Diet Coke and junk food, I started hot-gluing buttons to my wall (the Facilities Department was not amused). But mistakes can be good too: you'll never make the same mistake twice, but more important, you may end up learning something that you never expected. Honestly, I have always been a bit of a messy learner and I can only really figure things out by digging in and trying it myself. Developing your crafty self is really about developing your own creative processes. In other words, while there's often a wrong way to do something, there are many right ways.

I think it's time to stop talking and start crafting. I hope you enjoy making the projects in this book as much as I enjoyed dreaming them up. I encourage you to adapt them as much as you want or need. These are only starting points for your own creativity. Now go have some fun!

Tools and Techniques

This comprehensive section is full of useful techniques and step-by-step photographs and illustrations that are sure to set you on your way. Don't be afraid to expand on any of the topics covered. Be creative and you might impress yourself! From sewing and embroidering to beading and fabric painting, the myriad techniques included will allow you to become a crafty jack-of-all-trades.

Embellishing Basics

The first and most important part of embellishing is deciding what you would like to embellish. The possibilities are truly endless, so start looking around to see what you already have that can be improved, pressed back into service with a new use, or jazzed up a little just for fun!

Choosing Your Project

Look around. There are tons of boring old sweaters and faded T-shirts just begging to be reborn. Chances are, some of them are in your closet already. Thrift shops, yard sales, and clothing swaps are your next source. Think of all the items you see as works in progress. Tweed skirts look great with appliqués or bright ribbons, and shapeless men's shirts can be totally transformed with a few pintucks.

In this first chapter, you will find all of the information that you need about basic tools and materials that are used for all of the techniques and projects in this book. I have also covered all of the basic techniques that I use for the projects in detail with step-by-step instructions and either photographs or illustrations to illustrate each step.

The projects are divided into three sections: the first is garments; the second is accessories; and finally, items for the home are featured. Remember that you can mix and match ideas to your heart's content. An idea that I have used for a skirt could just as easily be applied to make an embellished tablemat. Don't be afraid to experiment—if something doesn't work out exactly as you intended it doesn't matter. And you never know—it may turn out even better!

As is the nature of embellishing, your projects will probably look very different from mine and so they should! Unless we shop at the same thrift stores or frequent similar flea markets (and if that's true, stop following me!) your finds will certainly not be exactly the same as mine. The projects featured in this book are really intended to be jumping-off points for you and your imagination. However, if you wish, you can follow exactly the designs, patterns, and templates that I have created for this book. Or you can simply use the technique, or a mixture of techniques, to create your own totally original designs.

You may have a good local source of embellishing supplies, but at the back of this book, you will find a list of resources that I use regularly to find my ribbons, trims, beads, and fabrics. Most of these are either nationwide stores, or web sites from which you can purchase the items.

Happy Embellishing!

Getting Started

Make sure you read the list of materials and all of the instructions thoroughly before you start a project. Like baking a cake, crafting requires you to be prepared and have everything you need to get the job done. That doesn't mean you shouldn't be creative— once you have some basic techniques down, I encourage you to find your own methods and shortcuts. I like to learn the "right" way to do things before I go off on my own path and try something new.

Your Embellishing Toolkit

For some projects you may need to buy special items, but tools and materials to always have on hand are:

Needles in different sizes: You'll want to have a variety of needles in different sizes for hand-sewing, embroidery, beading, and many other uses. If you want to get really organized, keep them in a needle book by type.

Straight pins: You can buy these with glass, plastic, or even flowered heads. I like to keep my pins in a pin cushion for accessibility.

Thread and embroidery floss: It's also nice to have a stash of basic colors in threads and flosses. When choosing a thread for a project, select one that is one shade darker than the dominant color in the project. You can usually get away with an all-purpose thread for most sewing projects, unless you are using very heavy or lightweight fabrics. I generally recommend avoiding the dollar-store variety of thread because it breaks and frays very easily.

Water-soluble pen or tailor's chalk: These are great tools for marking lines or drawing designs on fabrics. Water-soluble pens work better on cottons and tailor's chalk is more appropriate for fabrics with texture or fabric that the water-soluble ink might bleed into. For marking straight lines, you can also use masking tape.

Fusible webbing: Fusible webbing takes the fuss out of appliqué. You can buy webbing in sheets, by the yard (meter), or in rolls. You only need rolls if you plan on doing a lot of appliqué.

Fabric stabilizer: Fabric stabilizer stiffens fabric and helps keep fabric from moving around when you are embellishing it. You can purchase pin, iron-on, or self-stick stabilizers as well as stabilizers that tear away or dissolve in water. Stabilizer is essential when you are embellishing sheer or stretch fabrics.

Tracing paper: I use tracing paper for many different projects. It's useful when you want to alter an existing design or pattern. You can also trace patterns from this book and then alter them to better fit your garment. An 11 in. × 14 in. (27.9cm × 35.6cm) pad of 25 lb. tracing paper is sufficient for most needs.

Lightweight cardboard: This is essential when making pattern pieces. It isn't necessary to purchase cardboard; I make patterns using cereal boxes.

Bias tape makers: Never buy packaged bias tape again! You can make your own bias tape quickly and easily with these little tools. Bias tape makers come in sizes that make ¼ in. (6mm), ½ in. (13mm), ¾ in. (19mm), 1 in. (2.5cm), and 2 in. (5.1cm) finished-width double-fold bias tape.

Adhesives: Some of the adhesives I use regularly are fabric adhesive, jewelry adhesive, 5-minute epoxy, and hot glue. There are tons of different adhesives out there, so just make sure that you are buying the right one to get the job done.

Fabric and paper scissors: All scissors are not created equal! You don't have to buy the most expensive fabric scissors, but purchase a good-quality pair, and use them only to cut fabric. Paper scissors can be of lesser quality. To distinguish between the two, tie a small ribbon to the fabric scissors or mark them using a permanent marker. It is also nice to have small, sharp, pointed scissors for embroidery and for cutting threads. When I am working on a big project, I wear scissors around my neck on a ribbon so that I don't lose them amidst the piles of fabric.

Rotary cutter, straight edge, and cutting mat: A rotary cutter is indispensable for patchwork projects because you can accurately cut lots of identical pieces of fabric at the same time. Make sure you cut on a self-healing cutting mat. And use caution; rotary cutters are very sharp! I use a 45mm rotary cutter, 36-in. long (91.4cm) straight edge, and a 24 in. × 36 in. (61cm × 91.4cm) cutting mat.

Embroidery hoop: An embroidery hoop keeps an area of fabric stable and taut while you are embroidering. Unless you want your embroidery project to be all puckered and bumpy, I would recommend using one. An 8-in. (20.3cm) dia. hoop is good for most projects.

Planning Your Design

It is always a good idea to plan your design before you dig in. I think designing the project is always the most fun, so relish this process, and take as much time as you need. A well-planned design makes for a beautifully embellished project. Advance planning also means you will not be lacking a vital element halfway through the work, or suddenly find that you haven't considered the next step and need to backtrack on work already done.

Advance planning

Here are some techniques I use to plan a design:

Never underestimate the value of a sketchpad. Sometimes inspiration strikes on the way to work or sitting on the subway, so I keep one with me at all times.

A digital camera is handy for referencing designs. You can lay out your design first, and then as you're working, look back at the record photo to remember exactly where you pinned that flower or which color sequin goes where.

Make a list of all the ingredients needed for the project. Divide the list into items to purchase and items to gather. Put the items in one place and check them off the list before beginning.

Sewing

Most embellishing projects will require some sewing, either by hand or by machine. Although you can use fusible webbing or fabric adhesive to apply a few types of decoration, sewing is the key for a more professional look and a durable finish.

Hand-Sewing

Hand-sewing is the foundation of most embellishing projects and many of the projects in this book can be completed easily without a machine. I find hand-sewing to be very relaxing and meditative. The best part is you can take your project anywhere and work on it whenever you have a spare minute!

Running stitch

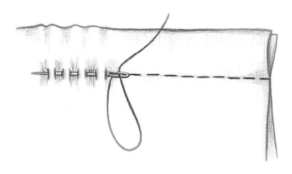

Slipstitch

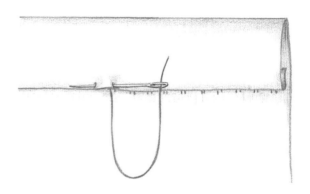

Hand-topstitching

Hand-sewing needles

Needles known as "sharps" can be used for most hand-sewing. They are moderately long with a small eye. If you have trouble threading a needle, use embroidery/crewel needles instead or purchase a needle threader. They come in the same lengths and weights as sharps but they have larger, oval eyes. Use sizes 3 and 7. The higher the number in hand-sewing needles, the thinner and shorter the needle.

Machine-Sewing

Sewing machines may seem daunting to novice crafters, but don't be intimidated! Get to know your machine and you will love all the things it can do for you. Even the most basic machines have several useful functions.

Straight stitch   **Small zigzag stitch**

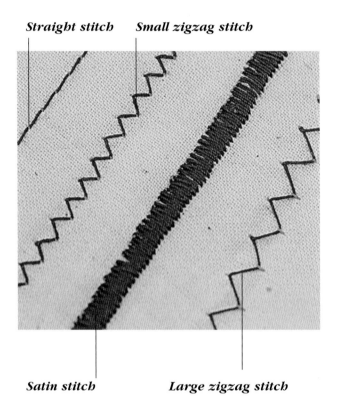

Satin stitch   **Large zigzag stitch**

Machine-sewing tips

If you don't know your machine that well, give your manual a good read. I consult mine whenever I need to learn how to use a new function.

All the projects in this book have ½-in. seam (13mm) allowance except where noted. The seam allowance is the area from the fabric edge to the stitching line.

The needle plate of your machine should have measurements for different seam allowances. If it doesn't, measure from the right of the needle, and put a strip of masking tape on the needle plate for the seam allowance you want.

After sewing a very curved seam, clip the seam allowance to ⅛ in. (3mm) of the stitching before turning the project right side out. This prevents weird bumps and gathers from developing in the seam. When a seam has a slight curve, the seam allowance should be trimmed to within 3/16 in. (5mm) of the seam and also be clipped.

Clip across a right-angle corner to ⅛ in. (3mm) of the stitching to eliminate bulk in the corner when the project is turned right side out.

Always use a sharp machine needle. A dull needle can cause missed stitches, especially on delicate fabrics or when doing machine embroidery. You can usually tell when a needle is dull; it makes a popping sound when it is sewing (as the blunt end of the needle tries to pierce the fabric). A good rule is to change your needle after each project.

Making Pockets

Adding extra elements to a garment is a great way to totally change the look. Follow these simple steps for great results every time.

1 Make a cardboard template of the pattern piece. Trace around template, and cut out fabric piece, lining, and interfacing.

2 Place lining right side up on interfacing. Place fabric piece right side down on lining. Pin all layers together.

3 Sew pieces together using ½ in. (13mm) seam allowance. Leave 3 in. (7.6cm) unsewn for turning. (See "Tips" on page 23.) Trim seam allowance to within ³⁄₁₆ in. (5mm) of seam. Clip curves and across corners. (See "Tips" on page 21.)

4 Turn right side out, pushing corners out using a chopstick or other pointed tool. Fold raw edges of opening to inside, and pin.

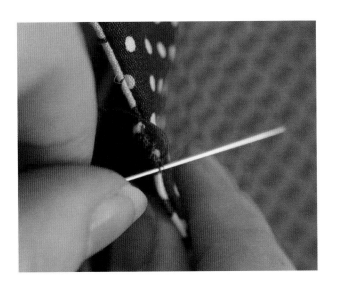 

5 Sew pinned opening closed using a whipstitch (shown here) or slipstitch. (See "Slipstitch" on page 20.)

6 You can either machine- or hand-topstitch ½ in. (13mm) from all edges if desired.

Sewing-machine needles

Size 10 or 12 universal needles are fine for most sewing. For machine needles, the higher the number, the thicker the needle. If you constantly have trouble with threads shredding, use a needle designed for metallic thread. It has a larger eye and a larger scarf (or channel) in which the thread lies when the needle is inserted into the fabric.

Needles remain sharp for only six to eight hours of sewing and then must be replaced.

Sewing tips

When sewing an item that will be turned right side out, plan for an opening at least 3 in. (7.6cm) long. Start at least ½ in. (13mm) from a corner and on an uncurved portion of the edge. Always backstitch twice at the beginning and end of sewing so that the seam doesn't open when turning an item.

Hand-topstitching is not only decorative, it keeps the edges neat so the piece stays nice and sharp. Omit this stitching if you want a less tailored look.

When working with large or complex pieces or with slippery fabrics, rather than pinning, it's better to baste the layers together before sewing. Basting holds the pieces more securely and sewing the item becomes less stressful for you.

Patchwork

I must confess that patchwork makes me dizzy with happiness. I love mixing patterns so that patchwork is a natural match for my aesthetic sensibilities.

1 To cut fabric for patchwork, you will need a rotary cutter, straight edge, and cutting mat. It's just so much easier and more precise than using scissors.

2 Use straight stitch and ¼-in. seam (6mm) allowance to sew small pieces together first. Then sew the large pieces, and complete the assembly.

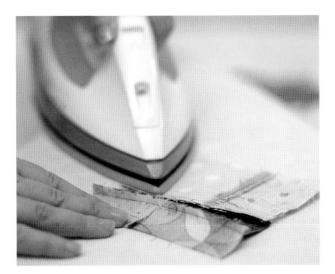

3 Always iron seams, either all to one side (toward darker fabric) or all open. There is a lot of debate as to which is the better method. I think it's up to the sewer, so find your preferred method, and stick with it!

Quilter's ruler

If you think you may become a serious quilter, it's worth investing in a 36-in. long (91.4cm) quilter's ruler. They are transparent, usually 6 in. (15.2cm) wide and are marked in a grid along with various lines for the angles that you encounter when making quilts. The quilter's ruler is the best straight edge to use because its wider width holds fabric securely when rotary cutting.

Sculpting Fabric

*One of the basic techniques in embellishing is to add texture and to change
the shape of the item with added sculptural features. Here's where yo-yos, ruffles,
and pleats come in!*

Yo-yos

Yo-yos are those cute little fabric puffs that look like rosettes. Though they were traditionally used for coverlets and have a country aesthetic, I think they can look quite modern and sculptural.

1 Cut a circle template twice the size of yo-yo desired, adding ¼-in. hem allowance (6mm). Use template and water-soluble pen to draw a circle on wrong side of fabric. Cut out fabric circle.

2 Thread needle, and knot thread end. With wrong side of fabric facing you, turn 1 in. (25mm) of hem to wrong side, and fold under ¼ in. (6mm). Insert needle into hem on side facing you, ⅛ in. (3mm) from fold. Make running stitches around circle, turning hem under as you sew.

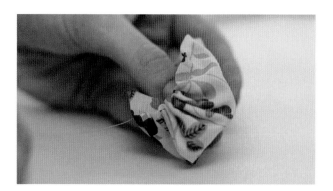

3 Pull thread to gather circle. Knot thread on inside hem. Center gathers on yo-yo, and iron.

Tighten up

For a tightly gathered yo-yo, use ¼-in. long (6mm) running stitches. For a more open center in the yo-yo, use running stitches that are ½ in. (13mm) long.

Ruffles

Ruffles are romantic embellishments to add to any project. They can be made out of fabric, ribbon, and other trims. You can use a ruffle foot on your sewing machine or this low-tech method. Make sure that you account for the amount of fabric that you will need: for sheer fabrics, measure the length of the area to which you are applying the ruffle, and multiply that measurement by three; for heavier fabrics, multiply the measurement by two.

Thread needle, and knot thread end. Start close to a short end, and make a running stitch ¼ in. (6mm) from long edge. Make running stitches the length of the ruffle. End close to other short end. Gently pull on thread to gather fabric to desired length. Knot thread to secure ruffle.

It's easy and fast to gather using a sewing machine. Adjust the stitch to the longest length. Begin by backstitching twice. Sew along long edge as for hand sewing. Do not backstitch at end. Cut thread ends to approximately 6 in. (15.2cm) long. Gently pull on bobbin thread to gather ruffle. Thread bobbin thread into a needle, and secure ruffle by knotting thread.

Pleats

There are so many different kinds of pleats, it would take up a whole book! For our purposes, we are just going to learn how to make a basic pleat.

Pleats can be made as wide as you would like, but be sure to measure accurately so they are even. For ½-in. pleats (13mm), make a ½-in. fold (13mm) and pin fold. Continue by making ½-in. folds (13mm) every 1 in. (2.5cm) to end of length, pinning each fold. Hand- or machine-sew ¼ in. (6mm) from pinned edge. Remove pins as you sew.

Embroidery

Embroidery is a perfect way to add a little something special to a ho-hum garment or to highlight another embellishment such as an appliqué. Most of the projects in this book use cotton embroidery floss, but you can also try ribbons, perle cotton, silk floss, or yarn.

Basic Embroidery

Embroidery can seem tricky, but it's a lot easier when you use the right tools! Stabilizer works wonders when embroidering on knits or delicate fabrics. Dressmaker's paper makes it a snap to copy your designs onto fabric. There are hundreds of different decorative stitches you can use, but here are a just a few of the basic ones to get you started. Remember, always use an embroidery hoop.

Split stitch

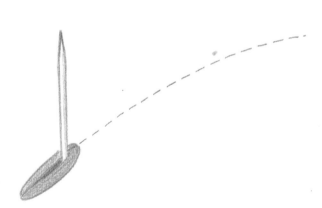

Blanket stitch

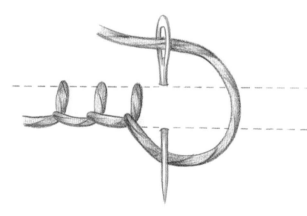

Transferring with chalk-backed dressmaker's paper
Copy design onto tracing paper or make a photocopy. Place tracing over fabric, and slip dressmaker's paper, chalk side down, under tracing. Pin both to fabric to prevent them from shifting while you work. Working on a hard surface, go over all lines using a sharp, hard pencil. Check that the image has transferred by lifting up a corner of the tracing and dressmaker's paper.

Backstitch

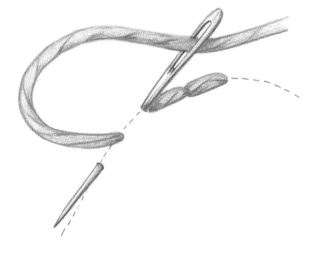

Satin stitch

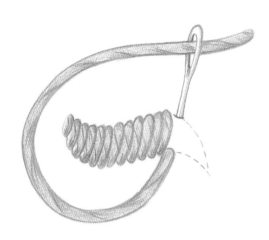

French knot

1

2

Chain stitch

1

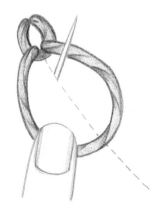

2

Cross stitch

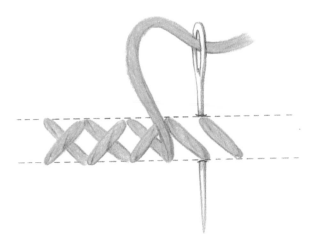

Laisy daisy stitch

Herringbone stitch

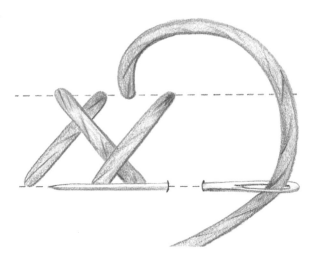

Feather stitch

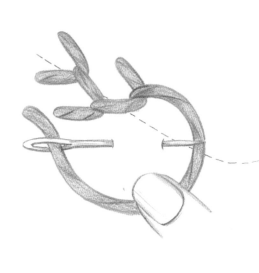

Hoops and needles

Use a hoop large enough for area being embroidered. Fabric should be tight in hoop and fabric weave should not be distorted. Tighten tension adjustment if there is one.

The best needles for embroidery are called embroidery/crewel. They have a large oval hole and a sharp point. For embroidery, use three or more strands of floss, and a size 7 needle. For fewer strands, use a size 8 needle.

Ribbon Embroidery

Ribbon embroidery has a romantic, old-fashioned feel that I really love. You can use many of the same stitches that you would for traditional embroidery, but the results will look different when using ribbon.

I use very narrow silk ribbons (2mm–4mm wide), which are available in a wide variety of colors. By twisting and looping the ribbons, you can also make realistic flowers. See "Folded Ribbon Roses" on page 36.

Running stitch

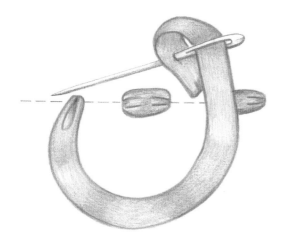

Spider web rose

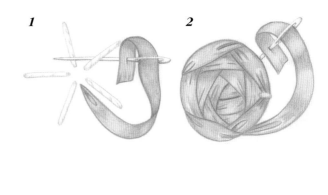

Twisted ribbon stitch

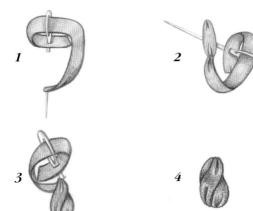

Ribbon stitch

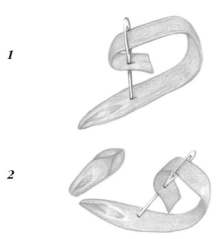

Basic couching

Fly stitch

1   **2**

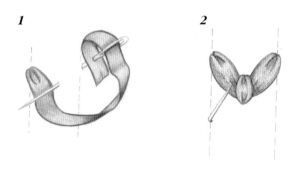

Gathered rosette

1

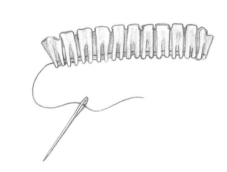

 2

A stitch in time

Use chenille needles for ribbon embroidery. They have a large oval eye and a sharp point. For 2mm- and 4mm-wide ribbons, use size 26; use size 24 for 7mm ribbon; and use size 18 for 13mm ribbon.

Needle size is important when doing ribbon embroidery. The width of the needle's eye makes a hole in the fabric, allowing the ribbon to pass through the fabric without fraying. The fabric hole will be too small when using a size 26 needle with wide ribbon. Using a size 18 needle with narrow ribbon will make a large hole that can be seen once the stitch is completed.

It's difficult to keep a needle threaded with ribbon because the ribbon easily slips out of the needle's eye. To prevent this, a special technique is used for securing ribbon in the needle. Thread ribbon end into needle. Insert needle into ribbon 1 in. (25mm) from ribbon end. Make a loose overhand knot close in free ribbon end.

Bring ribbon to wrong side of work when ending a strand of ribbon. Fasten ribbon end on wrong side with hand-sewing needle and matching sewing thread.

Folded Ribbon Roses

Here's a simple technique for making beautiful folded ribbon roses.

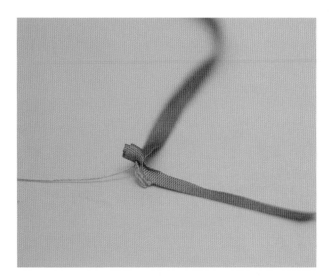

1 Thread hand-sewing needle with sewing thread to match color of ribbon; knot end; and set aside. Cut a 12-in. length (30.5cm) of 4mm ribbon. Fold 1 in. (2.5cm) of one end of ribbon toward you on a 45-deg. angle.

2 Roll diagonal fold onto longer end of ribbon five times to form center of flower. Sew through bottom edges of flower center to secure layers.

Using folded ribbon roses

Sew folded roses to your project by tacking the ribbon edges using matching sewing thread.

If you have the eyes and the patience, tiny folded roses can be formed from 2mm ribbon. The same technique can also be used to make roses from any ribbon width. Large roses made using 3-in. wide (7.6cm) wire-edge ribbon make wonderful gift-wrap decorations or are a lovely addition to a holiday wreath.

3 Fold longer end of ribbon away from you and on a 45-deg. angle. Roll flower center onto fold. Sew bottom edge to secure. Repeat by folding ribbon; rolling flower onto fold; and stitching. At the same time, roll the flower slightly higher each time to give depth to rose. Be sure to roll loosely. When flower is desired size, trim ends to ½ in. (13mm); tuck under rose; and tack to secure.

Duplicate Stitch

Duplicate stitch is an easy embroidery technique that mimics complicated intarsia knitting. Make sure that your item is knitted in stockinette stitch (the knit looks like a series of Vs), or this technique won't work.

1 You will need an item knitted in stockinette stitch; a size 16 tapestry needle; and a selection of contrasting color yarns the same thickness as yarn in knitted item. Thread needle with yarn, and knot.

2 Duplicate stitching is simply making V-shaped stitches over the existing V-shaped stitches on the knit. Bring needle from wrong side of knit to right side at bottom of a V.

3 Insert needle into top right end of V, and exit at top left end of V. Insert needle back into bottom of same V to complete stitch.

Plan ahead

To make a duplicate-stitch chart, copy a design onto graph paper. Each square on the graph paper equals one duplicate stitch.

Use a color pencil to represent each yarn color. Or, use a different symbol to represent each yarn color, such as +, −, x, or o. Make a key at the bottom of the graph paper, matching each symbol to a yarn color.

Determine where you want to locate the design on the knitted item. Mark the boundaries of the area using pins or basting stitches. It may be easier to work all of the outside stitches first and then fill in. Or, work an entire area in one color, and then move to the next—it's your choice.

Crochet

If you don't have the patience for crocheting entire garments, then crocheted embellishments are for you! Crochet is a great craft because it's entirely portable and requires just a couple of tools—a crochet hook and yarn. Hooks come in many different sizes, starting with the diminutive B (the smallest size) and going all the way up to a "giant" Q. Here are a few basic crochet techniques to get you started.

Foundation Chain

The first step in crochet is the foundation chain, which is the basis for all crochet stitches.

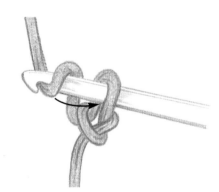

1 Make a slip knot by reeling off about a yard (meter) of yarn from the ball. Hold yarn in your palm 6 in. (15.2cm) from end. Using the yarn coming from ball, wrap yarn twice around your index and middle fingers. Pull strand coming from ball through loop between your two fingers, forming a new loop. Place this new loop on your hook. Tighten knot by pulling on free end of yarn. Adjust size of loop by pulling on yarn coming from ball until it fits hook.

2 To make the first chain stitch (ch st), wrap the yarn coming from the ball around the hook. This is called a yarn over (yo).

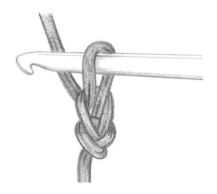

3 Use the hook to draw the yarn over through the loop of the slip knot. You have made one chain stitch! Continue to yarn over and draw the yarn through the loop on the hook for each remaining chain stitch needed for your project.

Slip Stitch

A slip stitch (sl st) has many important uses including: making drawstring cords and joining the ends of a foundation chain to form a ring for crochet motifs worked in the round.

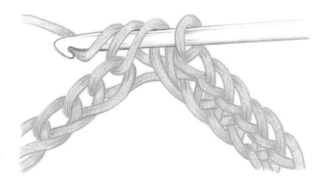

1 To make a drawstring cord, insert the crochet hook through both top loops of the first chain stitch from the hook. Yarn over the hook; then draw the yarn through the two top loops and the loop on the hook—one slip stitch has been made.

2 To join a foundation chain into a ring, insert the crochet hook through both top loops of the first chain stitch made. Yarn over the hook; then draw the yarn through the two top loops and the loop on the hook.

Fastening Off

After you have finished making your piece, cut off the remaining yarn, leaving an end of about 6 in. (15.2cm). Using the hook, pull this end through the last loop on the hook as if you were making a chain stitch, but pulling the end right through. Tighten the last loop to hold the end in place. If you want to use the end to sew up a seam, leave a much longer end before cutting off the excess yarn.

Blocking

It is essential to block your work if you want it to look its best. For blocking, you will need a spray bottle filled with warm water, straight pins, and a padded surface, such as a blocking board or padded ironing board. Form your crochet piece into the correct size and shape; then pin it down all around. Lightly mist over the entire piece with warm water until it is moist, but not soaked. Allow to air dry; then unpin.

Single Crochet

To work in single crochet (sc), the directions will ask you to crochet a foundation chain that has one more chain than the number of stitches needed for the project.

1 To make a single crochet stitch, insert the hook under the back loop of the second chain from the hook, then yarn over the crochet hook.

2 Now draw the yarn-over through the loop on the hook. You now have two loops on the crochet hook.

3 Yarn over the hook once more, then draw the yarn-over through the two loops on the hook.

4 You have made your first single crochet stitch. Continue to make a single crochet in each remaining foundation chain. For next and each row that follows, chain one and turn. You'll now be working through the two top loops of each single crochet stitch in the row below.

Half Double Crochet

To work in half double crochet (hdc), the directions will ask you to crochet a foundation chain that has two more chains than the number of stitches needed for the project.

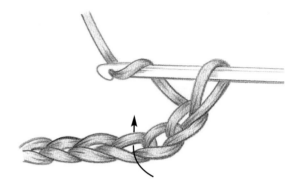

1 To make a half double crochet stitch, yarn over the crochet hook, then insert the hook under the back loop of the third chain from the hook.

2 Yarn over hook, then draw the yarn-over through. You now have three loops on the hook. Yarn over hook, then draw through all three loops on the hook.

3 You have made your first half double crochet stitch! Continue to make a half double crochet in each remaining foundation chain. For next and each row that follows, chain two, and turn. You'll now be working through the two top loops of each half double crochet stitch in the row below.

> ### Basic crochet abbreviations
> **beg:** begin, beginning
> **ch:** chain, chains
> **sl st:** slip st
> **sc:** single crochet
> **hdc:** half double crochet
> **dc:** double crochet
> **tr:** treble crochet
> **st/sts:** stitch/stitches
> **t-ch:** turning chain
> **yo:** yarn over
> **lp/lps:** loop/loops

Double Crochet

To work in double crochet (dc), the directions will ask you to crochet a foundation chain that has three more chains than the number of stitches needed for the project.

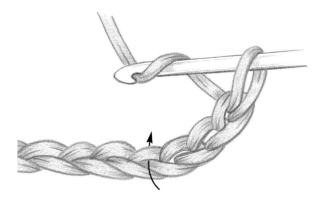

1 To make a double crochet stitch, yarn over the crochet hook, then insert the hook under the back loop of the fourth chain from the hook.

2 Yarn over hook, then draw the yarn-over through. You now have three loops on the hook. Yarn over hook, then draw through the first two loops on the hook.

3 You now have two loops on your hook. Yarn over hook once more, then draw the yarn-over through the last two loops on your hook.

4 You have made your first double crochet stitch. Continue to make a double crochet in each remaining foundation chain. For next and each row that follows, chain three, and turn. You'll now be working through the two top loops of each double crochet stitch in the row below.

Treble Crochet

To work in treble crochet (tr), the directions will ask you to crochet a foundation chain that has four more chains than the number of stitches needed for the project.

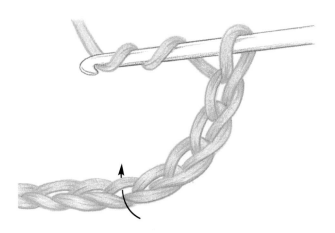

1 To make a treble crochet stitch, yarn over the crochet hook twice; then insert the hook under the back loop of the fifth chain from the hook.

2 Yarn-over hook, then draw the yarn-over through. You now have four loops on your hook. Yarn-over hook, then draw through the first two loops on the hook.

3 You now have three loops on your hook. Yarn over hook, then draw through the next two loops on the hook. You now have two loops on your hook. Yarn over hook once more, then draw through last two loops on your hook.

4 You have made your first treble crochet stitch. Continue to make a treble crochet in each remaining foundation chain. For next and each row that follows, chain four, and turn. You'll now be working through the two top loops of each treble crochet stitch in the row below.

Trims

Trims come in so many different types, shapes, and sizes that it is just impossible to cover them all here. Basic trim types include bias tape, ribbons, rickrack, braid, and lace.

Bias Tape

Bias-tape makers take the fuss out of creating your own custom tape, and the makers come in the five most popular sizes of tape. Because the fabric used for bias tape is cut on the bias, the tape has a built-in stretch that easily curves around garment edges.

Bias tape can be made from any fabric that holds a crease when ironed. It looks great sewn around a skirt hem or the edge of a napkin. Because it's easy to shape into curves and curlicues, it also makes lovely design motifs.

1 Open fabric right side down on cutting mat. Have selvedge (finished) edges at top and bottom. Fold top corner of fabric on a 45-deg. angle until fabric's cut edge matches bottom selvedge edge. Finger press fold. Open fold, and turn fabric, right side up.

2 Use fold as a guide for first cut. Follow bias-tape maker's instructions for fabric width needed. Cut strips using rotary cutter and straight edge. Cut one end of each fabric strip to a point. Insert fabric point into bias maker.

3 Press and pin fabric as it feeds through maker. To make double-folded bias tape, fold strip in half again, and iron.

On the bias

For some projects, you may need to sew several bias strips together to make one long strip before using the bias-tape maker. Trim the ends of each strip on a right angle. Place the strips, with right sides facing, on a 90-deg. angle to one another. Sew from the left corner of the top strip to the right corner of the bottom strip. Backstitch at the beginning and end of stitching. Trim $\frac{1}{2}$ in. (13mm) from stitching. Open strip, and iron seam open.

If you plan on laundering an item that has been decorated with bias tape, it's best to be sure that both the item and tape are washable. If either is not, dry cleaning is recommended.

Trimming tips

Find the right trim for the job. Heavy ribbons such as velvet brocades and grosgrains have very little flexibility so they can't be sewn around curves easily. Rickrack, bias tape, and many laces are suitable for sewing around curves.

You can also pleat and ruffle ribbons and laces using the same techniques as for fabric.

Another technique for embellishing with trims is to create your own trim by layering purchased trims. Sew a few narrow ribbons over a wider ribbon using decorative stitching, and you have a trim that is totally unique!

Ribbons, rickrack, and lace

There is a trimming store in the garment district in New York that is my idea of heaven. Trims, lace, and ribbons of all colors and sizes are displayed on shelves that reach the ceiling. On each visit, I find something that I have never seen before. Herein lies the appeal of trims: they aren't complicated to embellish with and there are so many available that you can customize each project according to your desires.

Ribbons and other trims

Making your own pleated trim

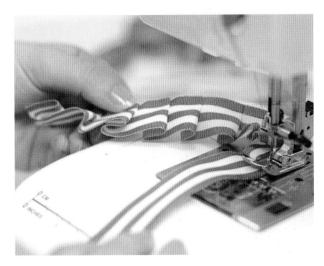

Felting

When most people think of felt, they picture those synthetic squares that kids use for craft projects, but wool felt is actually one of the oldest fabrics known. Wool felt is thick, tactile, and gorgeous. You can make your own wool felt, or you can buy wool felt by the yard. Felt can also be made from your hand-knitted or crocheted creations or by simply throwing a few old sweaters in the wash. You can also needle-felt using wool roving or wool yarn, and decorate garments or felted fabric.

Felting Sweaters and Other Wool Garments

If you have a sweater that doesn't fit or is full of holes and you want to sacrifice it to the crafty gods, here's what to do. Just throw your wool garments into the washing machine with a small amount of detergent.

Felting tips

If you only need pieces of the garment, cut up the garment before you felt it.

Hot water felts better than cold water, and putting the items in the dryer will felt wool even more. The best felting occurs when the wool fibers are really agitated, so it helps to throw something, such as an old pair of sneakers or a tennis ball, into the wash to really get things going.

You can put items to be felted in the washing machine for a short cycle, and take them out periodically to check on the felting process.

Once a garment is felted, it can be cut easily without the yarn raveling.

Felting works best when 100 percent wool garments are used. Yarn blends with no less than 60 percent wool will also felt, but the results aren't predictable.

Needle-Felting

You can needle-felt wool yarn, roving, or already felted fabric. You need a needle-felting tool (or single felting needles), needle-felting mat, and the wool material onto which you want to felt. I like to use a needle-felting tool for felting flat designs and single needles for more dimensional work.

Making flat designs

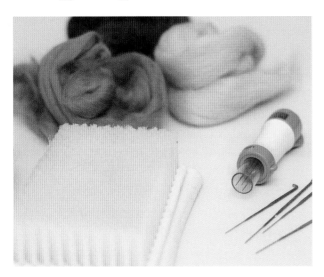

1 Set out your materials and tools. Decide on your design—let's say a circle.

2 Take a small amount of roving; twist the ends slightly, and coil to form a rough circle on the needle-felting mat.

3 Use your felting tool to punch into the roving while carefully using your fingers to sculpt the shape.

Heartfelt

I prefer to make my shapes on the felting mat first. Then I place the area of the garment to be needle-felted face up on the felting mat, and place the shape on it. I go over the entire shape again using the felting tool to secure, or felt, the shape to the garment.

Making dimensional designs

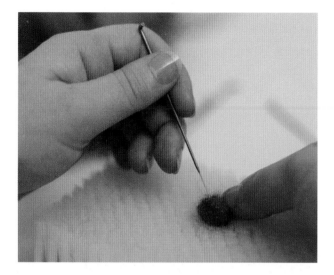

Roll a small amount of roving into a rough ball shape. Place ball onto the needle-felting mat. Use the single felting needle to shape it into a smooth ball, rolling and turning the ball as needed to felt it evenly.

Needle-felting tips

Dimensional designs can be needle-felted onto a garment with the single-felting needle. Working on the felting mat, punch the bottom-most portions of the design into the garment. Another method of securing the designs is to hand-sew them to the garment.

Cut-outs of previously felted fabric can be needle-felted onto a garment.

It's perfectly acceptable to needle-felt wool roving or yarn on a knitted garment that isn't 100 percent wool. In fact, the yarn needn't be 100 percent wool either.

Dry clean any garment that has been needle-felted even if it is washable. Needle-felting may loosen with the agitation and spinning of a washing-machine tub.

Using a stencil

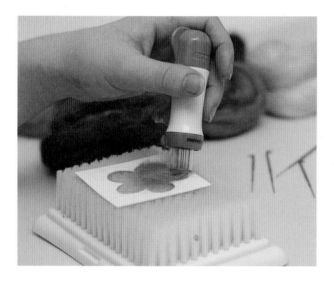

To make shapes, first cut a stencil out of cardboard. Then tape the stencil to the garment or tape it to the felting mat (if you wish to apply the shape to the garment after it has been needle-felted). Needle-felt, roving up to the edges of the stencil.

Doing line work

You can also use yarn to draw lines or make letters. Pin the yarn onto the project, and place it over the needle-felting mat. Punch the yarn with the felting tool, removing the pins as you work.

Beads, Baubles, and Sequins

For adding extra sparkle, nothing does the job like sequins and beads, and the best part is that you need only a few tools. To get started, you will need a water-soluble pen or tailor's chalk to mark your design on fabric. Most of the embellishment projects also require a needle and thread. If you are working on delicate or knit fabrics, you might want to add stabilizer to the back of the fabric, and place the backed fabric in an embroidery hoop.

Beads

Beads can not only be used to add sparkle, but also color, and a three-dimensional element to your designs. You can either add beads one at a time, or stitch on several at once.

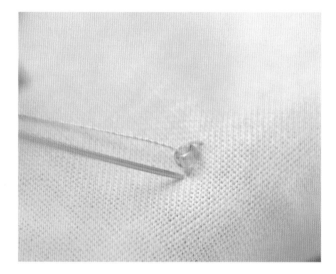

1 To sew on a single bead, insert needle from wrong side of fabric at point where you want bead to be secured. Thread bead onto needle, and with bead against fabric, insert needle into fabric on one side of bead.

2 Bring needle, through bead to right side of fabric. Insert needle into fabric on opposite side of bead. To add another bead, next to first, bring needle to right side of fabric, one-half bead width from first bead.

Adding multiple beads

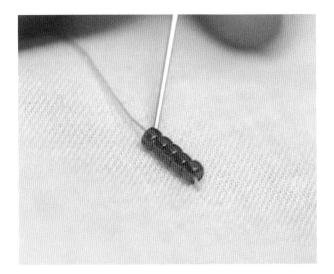

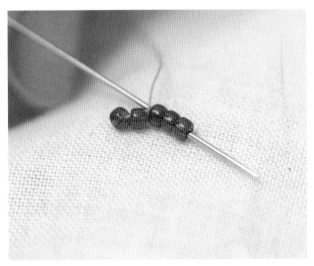

1 To sew multiple beads at once, bring needle up from wrong side of fabric. Thread five beads onto needle, and insert needle back down into fabric.

2 Bring needle back up through fabric between the second and third beads. Pass needle through third, fourth, and fifth bead. Add next group of five beads.

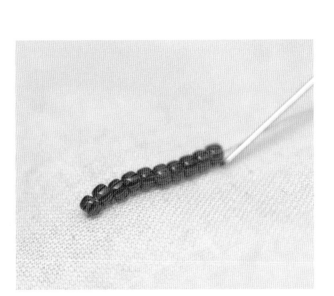

3 Continue adding beads five at a time until design is complete.

Bead savvy

A size 12 beading needle works well for all but the tiniest seed beads.

Seed beads are the tiniest beads available and come in a number of sizes. Size 6/0 (the largest), 8/0, and 11/0 are the most popular sizes. Pony beads look like seed beads but are larger and range from 8mm × 6mm to 9mm × 7mm. Glass, crystal, and gemstone beads can be round in sizes 3mm, 4mm, 6mm, 8mm, 10mm, 12mm, and 14mm, or they come in other shapes such as oval, bicone, rondelle, cube, double cone, etc.

D-weight thread is compatible with most bead sizes. Some beading threads are available in colors. When sewing beads onto fabric, choose a color that closely matches the fabric.

Buttons

While buttons often serve a utilitarian function, did you know that the first buttons to be used on clothing were purely for decoration? That's what we are going to be using buttons for in this book. If you don't want to sew on buttons, you can also glue them onto fabric or other materials using a permanent adhesive, such as jewelry adhesive.

Button up

Large decorative buttons are great, but make sure that the ones you choose are not too heavy for the weight of your fabric or the fabric will sag. This means that the button will hang face down instead of pointing nicely outward.

Some buttons have a shank on the back. This holds the button away from the surface of the fabric so a garment can be easily buttoned. If your button doesn't have a shank, and you are using it to fasten a garment or bag, etc., stitch it on quite loosely, then wind your thread a few times around the strands between the button and the fabric before fastening off.

Make your own custom buttons by layering small buttons on top of large ones; then sew or glue them together. If you want to sew layered buttons to a project, don't forget to line up at least two of the holes so you will be able to stitch through.

Sewing a button

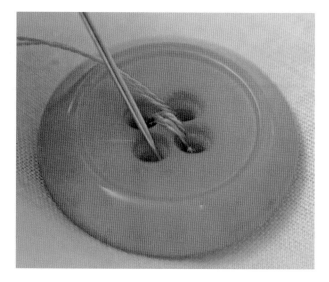

To sew on a button, thread a needle; double your thread; and make a knot at the end. Bring your thread from the back of the fabric, and sew through the holes of your button, securing through all layers. Repeat three or four times.

Flat-Back Jewels

These jewels come in many colors, shapes, and sizes, and can be glued, sewn on, or both. I prefer sew-on jewels, because I think they have a more finished look, but it does take a bit longer to add them to a design.

1 Arrange your design before you begin, and take a photo for reference.

2 Add a dot of jewelry adhesive (made for fabric) to the back of each jewel to keep them from shifting while you are sewing them on.

3 Double-knot thread in needle, and sew through each hole twice. End thread with knot on wrong side of fabric, and cut thread end. Repeat for each jewel hole.

Bejeweled

Flat-back jewels can be made of acrylic but the best ones are crystal. Crystal is worth the investment when you are designing a special project for yourself or as a gift because it reflects light better than acrylic.

Be sure the flat-back jewel you choose has a sufficient number of holes for secure sewing. Some have only one hole and those are used for hanging on jewelry.

The smallest, round crystal flat-back jewels, called montées, are mounted in silver-plated brass and range in size from 3.2mm to 6.4mm. There are thread holes in back of the brass fittings.

Studs

Studs have sharp, pointed prongs on the back. These prongs are inserted through the fabric and then bent to secure them. It is important to do this properly to avoid any scratches or injury.

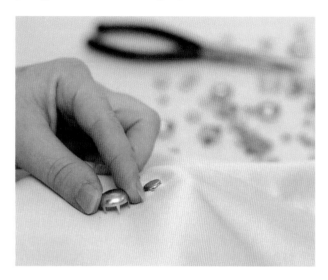

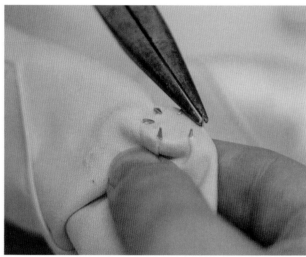

1 To set or secure studs, push prongs through fabric. Make sure all prongs push through and fabric is smooth and unwrinkled.

2 Use needle-nose pliers to first bend prongs at a 90-deg. angle to stud. Then curve point of each prong so it is inserted into fabric at center of stud.

Studs

The most popular sizes of studs are: 20 [$\frac{3}{16}$ in. (5mm)], 30 [$\frac{1}{4}$ in. (6mm)], 40 [$\frac{3}{8}$ in. (10mm)], and 60 [$\frac{1}{2}$ in. (13mm)].

There is a large range of stud shapes: round dome, round flat, faceted round, star, flower, heart, and many more. Studs come in metallic finishes of gold, silver, gunmetal, antique brass, copper, black, glitter, and colored enamel.

If you plan on using a lot of studs for projects, invest in a stud setter. This fairly inexpensive tool is easy to operate and will set sizes 20, 30, and 40 in much less time than doing it with pliers. It also sets pronged rhinestones.

Sequins

Sequins are a great way to add individual points of light or a sparkly line to a project. Sequins come in a range of shapes and sizes and can be either cupped or flat. Here are two ways to secure sequins.

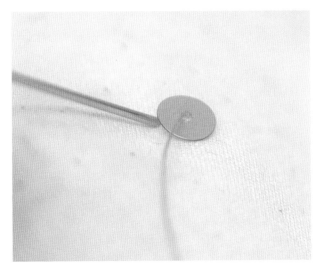

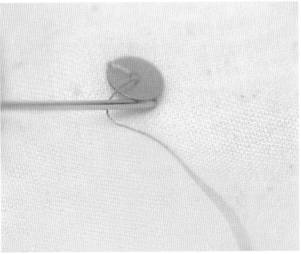

1 Thread needle, and knot thread end. Bring needle from wrong side of fabric and through sequin. Make a stitch close to outside edge of sequin.

2 Bring needle from wrong side of fabric through sequin. Make a stitch, opposite first stitch, close to outside edge of sequin.

Using a bead

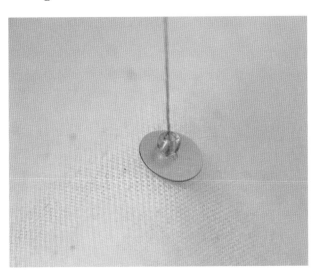

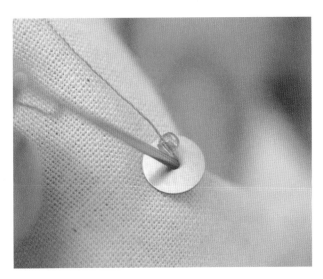

1 Bring needle from wrong side of fabric through sequin and bead.

2 Insert needle back into sequin and through fabric. The bead secures the sequin to the fabric. If it has a small hole, you will need to use a beading needle.

Appliqué

Appliqué, from the French word appliqué, meaning "to apply," is an ancient needlework technique in which one layer of fabric is sewn to another, usually a foundation fabric. Appliqué has come a long way since the invention of fusible webbing. You can use webbing to fuse fabric to a foundation fabric before stitching.

Basic Appliqué

With basic appliqué, fabric shapes in different colors are applied on top of a foundation fabric.

1 Place fabric right side down. Use an iron to fuse webbing, paper side up, to fabric.

2 Draw design on paper side of webbing, and cut out shape. You can also trace design onto paper side of webbing before fusing it to fabric.

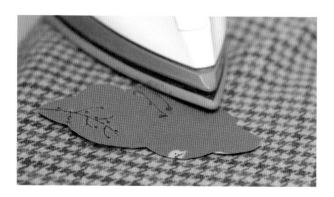

3 Remove paper backing, and use an iron to fuse shape to foundation fabric.

4 Embroider, using an embroidery hoop, or machine-sew outline of design.

Reverse Appliqué

In reverse appliqué, a contrasting fabric is applied to the wrong side of the foundation fabric. The design outline is stitched, and then the foundation fabric is cut away close to the stitching lines.

1 Draw appliqué design on right side of foundation fabric (denim in this case). Pin contrasting appliqué fabric, face up, behind foundation fabric.

2 Embroider using an embroidery hoop, or machine-sew outline of design.

3 Carefully cut away foundation fabric along inner edge of stitching. Remove pins.

Appliqué notes

Embroidery stitches to use when outlining appliqué are: split stitch, backstitch, or chain stitch. Sewing-machine stitches to use are: satin stitch, buttonhole stitch, or zigzag.

Most fusible webbings are strong enough to hold appliqués without sewing the edges, but sewing really finishes the piece and takes your work to the next level.

Reverse appliqué works best when the foundation and contrasting appliqué fabrics are the same weight. If you have your heart set on an appliqué fabric that is lighter weight than the foundation fabric, iron fusible interfacing on the wrong side of the appliqué fabric to give it more weight.

Fabric Printing

Printing images on fabric adds a new dimension and texture to garments and home accessories. There are several different ways to accomplish this look, including stencils, stamping, image transfers, and embossing.

Potato Printing

Potato prints are not just for child's play. Potatoes can yield modern, graphic prints that are perfect for fashion and home décor projects. The best thing about potato printing is it's an inexpensive technique.

1 Cut potato in half lengthwise, and chill in the fridge for an hour. Blot up excess moisture using paper towel.

2 Use black fine-tip permanent marker to draw design onto cut surface of potato. Use lino cutter to cut around the design, removing all areas that should not print to about ⅛ in. (3mm) deep.

It's all in the fine print

When printing on fabric make sure you use a permanent fabric ink. Follow the manufacturer's directions to heat set the design with an iron.

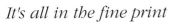

Always allow the ink to dry thoroughly before heat setting.

To turn acrylic paint into permanent paint for fabric, combine it with fabric-painting medium, following proportions on label.

3 Use small sponge to apply fabric ink evenly onto potato. Firmly press potato onto surface to be printed.

Freezer-Paper Stencils

Freezer paper wasn't designed for stencils, but it's a great way to make stencils that will be used only a few times. Because it's inexpensive, you can try out lots of ideas.

1 Draw design on matte side of freezer paper. Have at least 2-in. border (5.1cm) of paper on all sides. Working on cutting mat, cut out design using craft knife.

2 With shiny side of freezer paper face down, iron stencil onto right side of fabric using dry iron. Make sure stencil adheres completely.

3 Use small sponge brush to dab ink onto stencil. Don't brush on ink or it will run under edges of stencil.

4 Once entire design has been stenciled with ink, peel off stencil.

Image Transfers

Ahh, the wonders of modern technology. Image transfers allow for the printing of computer-generated designs or photos onto fabric. There are many kinds of transfer papers for different types of applications. Be sure you read the manufacturer's directions to ensure your printer is compatible with the paper.

1 Print image on transfer paper. Cut out, leaving a ½-in. border (13mm) on all sides.

2 Place fabric, right side up, on a smooth, hard surface (not an ironing board). Position transfer, face down. Following the manufacturer's directions, iron the transfer.

3 Let cool; then peel corner of transfer paper off carefully to check that image has been completely transfered. If it hasn't, go over area again with iron.

Image makers

Because a transfer is placed on the fabric, face down, any lettering in the design will be backwards on the fabric. To avoid this, make a flipped or flopped photocopy of the image and use that to print the transfer.

Transfers work best on fabrics with a smooth finish. Heavily woven fabrics, such as denim, can be used but the texture of the fabric may break up any fine lines in the design. For those types of fabric use bold designs with large, solid areas of color.

Embossing on Velvet

Have you ever looked at those gorgeous embossed velvet scarves and wondered, "How in the world did they do that?" Actually the process is easy. You can use rubber stamps, or even thick lace to emboss patterns into velvet. Add a water mister, an iron, and a water-soluble pen, and you're ready to emboss.

1 Mark placement of design motifs on wrong side of fabric. Place fabric, right side (pile side) down, over embossing motif. Mist wrong side of fabric.

2 Hold dry iron, set on "rayon," over fabric for ten seconds without moving it. Do not iron back and forth. This will cause the image to be blurry. Change position of iron, and iron again for another ten seconds. You will see embossed design appear on wrong side of fabric.

3 Lift fabric. Design is now embossed onto surface of velvet.

Velvet revolution

Garment-weight rayon velvet is the only choice for embossing. Cotton velvet will not emboss and while upholstery-weight velvet will emboss with effort, it's too heavy for most projects and quite pricy. It's also best to use medium- or dark-colored velvets. Embossing is not effective on light-colored velvets because it's difficult to see the embossing.

Dyeing Fabric

Each fabric dye is different and may require hot or cold water and salt or other additives.

Dyeing Tips

Make sure the dye is right for your fabric. All-purpose fabric dyes work best on natural materials. You can also buy dyes specifically for silks or synthetics.

Make sure you protect your clothes, skin, and work area from the dye; cover everything with plastic; and make sure to wear gloves!

If you are dyeing a project with multiple colors, it is usually best to dye the palest color first, then work up to the darkest.

You can get unusual effects by masking some areas so that they will not take the dye at all, or not as well as other areas. You can mask by painting areas with wax (which will come out when the item is washed in hot water) or by tying sections of the fabric up tightly, which gives a tie-dye effect.

Submerge the fabric in clean, warm water first. This helps the dye adhere to the fabric more evenly once it is in the dye bath.

Make sure the dye has been fully dissolved, and stir well before you submerge your fabric or there will be little spots of darker color on your fabric. Keep on stirring after the fabric has been submerged to make sure that all of it gets an even coverage.

Most dyeing can be done with basic kitchen equipment, but keep tools that are strictly for dyeing separate, and label them well. When dyeing, be mindful of children or pets. You don't want them touching or accidentally ingesting any dyes.

Painting and Etching

Next time you are in your craft- or art-supply store, familiarize yourself with the different types of paints offered. For lasting results, it's best to use the right paint, ink, or other supply for a project. Don't use a substitute in the hope that it will work. If you want a decorative effect that's a great alternative to painting on glass, try etching.

Painting wisdom

Don't use artists tube-acrylic paints for craft projects. They are more expensive and don't cover as well as craft acrylics.

There are special paints formulated for painting on glass and ceramics. They are food and dishwasher safe once they are heat set in the oven. Be wary of using other paints for dishes or glassware.

Stick with one brand of paint. Then you can be sure that the fabric-painting medium, crackle medium, etc., that the paint company makes will be chemically compatible with their paint. Don't use acrylics (which are water based) with oil-based paints or varnishes. You will get unexpected and unwanted results.

Craft acrylics can be used on wood, metal, paper (which may buckle if applied too heavily), or fabric. Read the manufacturer's instructions, and be aware that for some applications, a special medium must be mixed with the paint or the paint will not adhere properly.

Etching

Once upon a time, glass was etched with highly corrosive acids. Now you can get similar results by using etching cream, available in any craft store. This is a fun and easy way to decorate your glassware.

1 Cut a piece of translucent self-stick vinyl slightly larger than design. Slip design under vinyl, and trace using black fine-tip permanent marker.

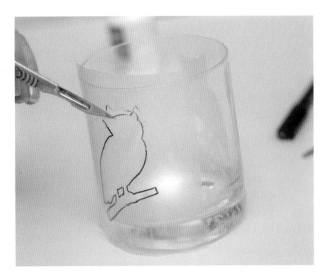

2 Use rubbing alcohol to clean area to be etched. Do not touch this area with your fingers. Peel off backing paper, and apply vinyl to glass. Use very sharp craft knife to cut out design. Remove vinyl from design area. Cover your finger with a clean cloth, and smooth cut edges of design firmly to glass.

3 Following manufacturer's directions, brush a thin layer of etching cream on design area. Wait specified amount of time, then rinse glass under running water, and peel off vinyl. When glass is dried, your etched design will be visible.

Etch 'n' sketch

The oils in your fingers will stop the etching cream from working. After cutting out the design and before etching, check design area on the glass for finger smudges. Use cotton swabs and rubbing alcohol to wipe away smudges. Don't allow the alcohol to touch the edges of the vinyl—it will dissolve the vinyl's adhesive.

Wear gloves, protect your work surface and clothing, and work in a well-ventilated area when etching.

Garments

Clothes are the most popular items for embellishing.
Everyone has a tired piece of clothing they would like to
give a new lease of life. Or hunt through flea markets, swap
meets, or local thrift shops for a likely item to embellish and
make into a star member of your wardrobe.

Yo-yo Yoke Blouse

Yo-yos often conjure up visions of vintage country quilts, but their shape can be sculptural and modern. I used yo-yos on a silk blouse with a yoke for this project. If you have a strappy, sleeveless top that doesn't have a yoke, simply cut off the straps; sew yo-yos together to make straps; and then use yo-yos to frame the neckline.

Materials

Pencil compass
Lightweight cardboard
Pencil
Ruler
Paper scissors
¼ yd. (.25m) each of three cotton prints
¼ yd. (.25m) of solid cotton
Water-soluble pen
Fabric scissors
Sleeveless silk blouse with yoke
Straight pins
Hand-sewing needle
Matching sewing thread
Iron

Ups and downs

For a subtle design, choose fabrics that match the color of the blouse. For a more outrageous look, use highly contrasting colors.

Alternatively, if it's fabric texture that interests you, make the yo-yos in the same or similar fabric to the blouse.

You can also make yo-yos lined in a contrasting color. Cut a second circle of fabric half the diameter and minus the seam allowance of the yo-yo. Place the lining in the center of the yo-yo. Gather the yo-yo using very short stitches. This will allow for a larger opening in the center, and the lining will be visible.

Step 1 Use pencil compass to draw four circle templates onto cardboard: 2½-in. dia. (6.4cm), 3½-in. dia. (8.9cm), 5-in. dia. (12.7cm), and 6½-in. dia. (16.5cm). Cut out templates using paper scissors.

Step 2 Use templates to trace several circles of each size onto each fabric. Cut out fabric circles using fabric scissors. Number of yo-yos you need will depend on your blouse. I used 1 extra-large, 4 large, 14 medium, and 16 small yo-yos.

Step 3 See "Yo-yos" on page 26 for yo-yo making technique.

Step 4 Place extra large yo-yo at center bottom of front yoke. Pin yo-yos on either side as shown. Make sure yo-yo yoke is symmetrical and covers blouse yoke completely. Pin yo-yos to each other, and unpin from blouse.

Step 5 Use needle and thread to sew yo-yos together on wrong side. Make sure stitching can't be seen on right side.

Step 6 Pin yo-yo yoke to blouse. With wrong side of blouse face up, sew yo-yo yoke to blouse.

Step 7 You can also add yo-yos scattered over rest of blouse for a more organic look. Turn blouse to right side.

Step 8 To retain their dimensional appearance, don't flatten yo-yos when you iron blouse.

Vintage Appliqué Dress

If you have ever spent any time at a flea market, you have probably noticed piles and piles of lovely embroidered vintage linens for sale. These linens are a powerful connection to our past and a reminder of the beauty people once crafted into their everyday possessions. Unfortunately, this also means that these linens often come with stains along with the wear-and-tear of daily use. The Vintage Appliqué Dress is one way to re-use these well-worn treasures.

Materials

Assorted pieces of embroidered vintage linens

Iron

Surplice necklined dress in cotton

Tape measure

Fabric scissors

Fabric adhesive

Hand-sewing needle

Matching sewing thread

Dress form (optional)

Seed beads in desired colors

Beading needle

Matching beading thread

A little shortcut…

Using vintage linens is a quick way to incorporate beautiful embroidery into your embellishing projects. The time-consuming work of embroidering is already done for you!

Step 1 Check your collection of embroidered linens, and make sure they're clean. Iron them if they're wrinkled.

Step 2 Measure edges of surplice neckline. Select an interesting embroidery border, and cut two strips to length of each neckline edge. Have about ¼ in. (6mm) of fabric on either side of border. Dot back of strips with fabric adhesive, and apply strips to neckline.

Step 3 Find an embroidered motif that measures about 4 in. long × 3 in. wide (10.2cm × 7.6cm). Cut out, leaving about ¼-in. border (6mm) on all sides. Dot back with fabric adhesive, and apply to dress on right shoulder.

Step 4 Find motif that is about 9 in. long × 5 in. wide (22.9cm × 12.7cm). Cut out, leaving about ¼-in. fabric (6mm) border around embroidery. Dot back with fabric adhesive, and apply to right side of dress at waistband, wrapping it slightly around side of dress.

Step 5 Try dress on to be sure that it's still comfortable and that you don't need to adjust position of any motifs.

Step 6 Thread sewing needle, and knot end. Secure neckline border and motifs to dress with running stitches, sewing within ¼-in. wide (6mm) border. This step is easier if you have a dress form, although be careful not to stitch into it as you work. (See "Running stitch" on page 20.)

Step 7 Decide where you want seed-bead accents. I used red and yellow beads to accent flowers at waist, green beads for leaves at neckline, and pink beads for bow at shoulder. You can add as many or as few beads as you like.

Step 8 Thread beading needle with beading thread, and knot end. Sew on seed beads. (See "Beads" on page 50.)

Quick fixes

I really like the shabby-chic effect that embroidery motifs give when they begin to fray. If you prefer a cleaner look, you can apply a small amount of fray-preventive liquid to the edges of each motif before you sew them to the dress.

Using the same technique but with a slightly different look, cut out motifs from a fabric with a large floral print, and machine-stitch them to the dress.

If you're really short on time, you can purchase premade embroidered motifs, and sew them to your dress instead.

Mod Squad Tee

Thrifting addicts like myself often have a running list in our heads of things to look for when shopping. I have always been a sucker for shirts with giant collars and crazy prints. The problem is that they are usually made of synthetic fabric, which doesn't breathe at all. This embellished cotton T-shirt is a nice alternative. It has all the style of a vintage top but with a lot more comfort.

Materials

Paper scissors
¼ yd. (22.9cm) of print fabric
¼ yd. (22.9cm) of solid fabric
¼ yd. (22.9cm) of lightweight interfacing
Straight pins
Fabric scissors
Sewing machine
Matching sewing thread
Iron
Scoop neck T-shirt in cotton
Hand-sewing needle
Tailor's chalk
Button-covering kit (if required)
Seven self-cover buttons, ½-in. dia.(13mm)
⅝ yd. (.57m) of ½-in. wide (13mm) velvet ribbon
⅔ yd. (.60m) of ⅜-in. wide (10mm) velvet ribbon
Fabric adhesive

Step 1 Enlarge collar pattern on page 171 to 300% or desired size. Cut out pattern using paper scissors.

Step 2 Fold print fabric in half with wrong sides facing. Place pattern on fold, and pin. Cut out using fabric scissors, and remove pins. Repeat with solid fabric and interfacing.

Step 3 Place solid fabric right side up on interfacing. Place print fabric right side down on solid fabric. Pin all layers together.

Step 4 Pin collar to neck of T-shirt. Trim off any excess collar fabric along neckline. Unpin collar from T-shirt.

Step 5 Machine-stitch around collar edges, leaving 3-in. opening (7.6cm) at center back. Trim seams and clip corners. (See "Tips" on page 21.)

Step 6 Turn collar right side out. Turn edges of opening to inside, and pin closed. Hand-sew opening using slipstitch. (See "Slipstitch" on page 20.)

Step 7 Machine-sew topstitching around collar ½ in. (13mm) from edge. Use tailor's chalk to mark center back of collar.

Mods and rockers

Feel free to experiment with trims on this project: grosgrain ribbon, rickrack, or vintage lace would all look great.

Adding a collar is a great way to totally change the look of a top. You can even make several alternative collars in different fabrics, and attach them with snaps (poppers) instead of sewing them on. Then you can change the collar to match several different outfits.

We show a purchased belt in the photograph, but it is quite easy to make a wide belt to match your collar. Measure your waist, and add 6 in. (15.2cm). Cut fabric to that length by 7 in. (17.8cm) wide. Fold the fabric strip in half with right sides facing and matching the long edges. Machine-stitch one short end and the long edge. Trim the seam allowances close to the seamline and turn right side out. Tuck the raw edges of the unsewn end of the belt to the inside. Fold this end around the center shank of a pull-through buckle. (Don't use a buckle with a prong unless you have an eyelet-setting kit. You would need to make holes for the prong in the other end of the belt.) Hand-sew across the end around the shank to secure the belt to the buckle.

Step 8 Find center front and center back of T-shirt neckline, and mark with tailor's chalk. Pin collar to neck edge of T-shirt. Match center back of collar with center back of neck on T-shirt.

Step 9 Hand-sew collar to T-shirt using slipstitch.

Step 10 Using a button-covering kit (if required) and following manufacturer's directions, cover seven buttons with print fabric.

Step 11 Cut two 4½-in. (11.4cm) lengths of ½-in.-wide (13mm) ribbon for sleeve detail. Fold one end of each ribbon length under ½ in. (13mm), and apply a tiny amount of fabric adhesive on wrong side to secure.

Step 12 Use tailor's chalk to mark edge of each sleeve at center point opposite underarm seam. Pin ribbons to center point (as shown in photograph on page 75) with turned-under top of ribbons 3 in. (7.6cm) from edge of sleeves. Turn other end of ribbons 1 in. (2.5cm) under sleeve edges.

Step 13 Machine-stitch ribbons to sleeve, close to both edges of ribbon.

Step 14 As shown in photograph, hand-sew two covered buttons to ribbon on each sleeve.

Step 15 Cut one 7-in. length (17.8cm) and two 4-in. lengths (10.2cm) of ½-in.-wide (13mm) ribbon. Cut two 6-in. (15.2cm) lengths of ⅜-in. wide (10mm) ribbon.

Step 16 Pin ribbons to front of T-shirt. For all ribbons, fold top 1-in. (2.5cm) end onto wrong side of T-shirt. Pin 7-in. length (17.8cm) to center front. Pin two 6-in. lengths (15.2cm) on either side of center ribbon. Pin two 4-in. lengths (10.2cm) on either side of last ribbons pinned.

Step 17 Machine-stitch ribbons to T-shirt, allowing some of the ribbon ends to hang free. Cut center ribbon end into dovetail and cut others at an angle.

Step 18 Hand-sew remaining three buttons to center ribbon.

Buttons

You can use purchased buttons instead of self-cover buttons on this tee. Choose washable buttons in colors that complement or contrast with the print fabric, depending on how bold you want the effect to be.

Victoriana Cardigan

Did you ever imagine your boring old cardigans had this kind of potential? This ruffled and trimmed cardigan has been completely transformed with the help of felted sweater scraps from my felt stash. I love working with felted wool. The felting process shrinks the wool fibers so that no hemming is needed and felted wool stretches nicely so it is an easy fabric to use for embellishing.

Materials

V-neck cardigan in wool

Embroidery scissors

Tape measure

Rotary cutter, straight edge, and cutting mat

Three felted sweaters or scraps from your felted-
    sweater stash

Sewing machine

Matching sewing thread

Hand-sewing needle

Straight pins

Dress form (optional)

Three sets of hook-and-eye fasteners

Needle-felting mat

Single needle-felting needle

Small amount of wool roving in two colors

Fabric scissors

Step 1 Remove buttons from cardigan using embroidery scissors.

Step 2 With cardigan front facing you, measure front opening, from bottom edge on left side, around neck to bottom edge on right side.

Step 3 Working on cutting mat using rotary cutter and straight edge, cut strips of felted sweater 2½ in. (6.4cm) wide. (See Felting on page 46.) For gathering, final strip must be twice the length in step 2. Cut a sufficient number of strips and machine-sew together using ½ in. (13mm) seams.

Step 4 Thread sewing needle with thread cut to length in step 2 plus 18 in. (45.7cm). Sew running stitches along one long edge strip. Pull thread to gather strip into a ruffle to length in step 2. Knot thread to hold gathers. (See "Running stitch" on page 20.)

Step 5 Align end of ruffle with inside bottom edge on left side of cardigan. Have cardigan edge overlap gathered edge of ruffle by ½ in. (13mm). Pin ruffle around opening, ending at bottom edge of right side.

Step 6 Machine-sew ruffle to cardigan using straight stitch.

Step 7 Add 2 in. (5.1cm) to measurement in step 2.

Step 8 Using rotary cutter and straight edge, cut 1-in. wide (2.5cm) strips of felted sweater. Cut and sew several strips together to make length in step 7. I sewed two different colored strips together for added interest, but you may choose to use just one color.

Step 9 Pin 1-in. wide (2.5cm) strip to right side of cardigan, turning end of strip 1 in. (2.5cm) to wrong side of cardigan. Have strip begin at bottom edge of left side. Pin around opening, covering button holes, and ending at bottom edge of right side. Turn end of strip to wrong side of cardigan.

Step 10 Adjust sewing machine for a small zigzag stitch. Sew along both edges of strip.

Step 11 Put cardigan on dress form, if available, or try on cardigan. Use straight pins to mark three points where cardigan will fasten. Hand-sew three hook-and-eye fasteners to cardigan.

Making the flower

Step 1 Roll a small amount of roving into a rough ball. (See "Making dimensional designs" on page 48.)

Step 2 Place ball onto needle-felting mat. Use felting needle to shape it into a neat ball, rolling and turning ball as needed to felt it evenly. Make six balls, either in same color or in different colors as desired. Set balls aside for the moment.

Step 3 Using rotary cutter and straight edge, cut a strip of felted sweater 2½ in. wide × 16 in. long (6.4cm × 40.6cm).

Step 4 Use fabric scissors to cut scallop-shaped petals into one long edge of strip. (See photograph.)

Step 5 Using rotary cutter and straight edge, cut a contrasting strip 2 in. wide × 24 in. long (5.1cm × 61.0cm).

Step 6 Cut scallop-shaped petals into one long edge of strip.

Step 7 Sew running stitches along uncut edge of each strip. Gather strips to about half their original length, when they start to curl.

Step 8 Form 2½-in. wide (6.4cm) strip into a rosette and hand-sew layers together at base. Repeat with 2-in. strip (5.1cm). Place it on 2½-in. strip (6.4cm) and hand-sew together.

Step 9 Hand-sew felt balls to center of flower.

Step 10 Hand-sew flower to right side of cardigan.

Layer Cake T-shirt

Rows of ruffles and pleats always remind me of layer cakes because they are so deliciously feminine. This type of top always looks best when paired with your tightest jeans and boots, which add an edge to all that sugary sweetness. If your jersey fabric only stretches in one direction, make sure to cut it so the stretch runs across the T-shirt and not up and down, or you might have a hard time pulling the T-shirt over your head!

Materials

T-shirt (loose fitting)
Tailor's chalk
Tape measure
Paper
Pencil
½ yd. (.46m) each of two cotton jersey fabrics
Rotary cutter, straight edge, and cutting mat
Sewing machine
Matching sewing thread
Straight pins
Fabric scissors
3 yds. (2.7m) of 1-in. wide (2.5cm) stretch lace
3 yds. (2.7m) of ¼-in. wide (6mm) elastic
Dress form (optional)
Hand-sewing needle

Step 1 Put on T-shirt, and use tailor's chalk to mark your waistline.

Step 2 Measure 3½ in. (8.9cm) down T-shirt from first mark, and mark again. Have a friend measure around T-shirt at each mark, making sure tape measure is not pulled too tightly.

Step 3 Multiply each measurement by 2 and add 2 in. (5.1cm) to each. Write measurements down, noting first one as "waist" and second one as "hips."

Step 4 Working on cutting mat and using rotary cutter and straight edge, cut strips from cotton jersey. For pleats at waist, cut one strip 1½ in. (3.8cm) wide and one strip 2½ in. (6.4cm) wide. Both strips should be length noted in step 3.

Step 5 For pleats at hips, cut one strip 1½ in. (3.8cm) wide, one strip 2½ in. (6.4cm) wide, and one 4-in. wide (10.2cm) strip. All strips should be length determined in step 3. You may need to sew strips together, using ½ in. (13mm) seam allowance, to get desired length.

Step 6 Machine-sew ½-in.-long (13mm) pleats every 1 in. (2.5cm) on all strips. If you want exact pleats, measure and pin strips before sewing. Or you can just estimate. (See "Pleats" on page 29.)

Step 7 With right sides face up and sewn edges aligned, layer 1½ in. (3.8cm) waist pleat over 2½ in. (6.4cm) waist pleat, and pin. Machine-sew together along stitching line.

Step 8 With right sides face up and sewn edges aligned, layer 1½-in. (3.8cm) hip pleat over 2½-in. (6.4cm) hip pleat. Layer both over 4-in. (10.2cm) hip pleat, and pin. Machine-sew together along stitching line.

Step 9 Cut two pieces of lace without stretching it. Cut one to length of waist pleats and one to length of hip pleats. Pin lace to top of each pleated strip on right side. Have bottom edge of lace overlapping pleat stitching line ¼ in. (6mm). Machine-sew close to bottom edge of lace.

Step 10 Cut two pieces of elastic without stretching it. Cut one to length of waist pleats and one to

Layers, layers, layers
For the ultimate in romance, skip the jersey fabric and pleat yards of stretch lace in different widths and colors.

Another cool option is to choose solid jersey fabrics in graduated shades. Start with the lightest as the first pleat and continue down the T-shirt with gradually darker colored pleats.

length of hip pleats. Pin to top of lace on wrong side. Machine-sew elastic to lace using widest, medium-length zigzag stitch.

Step 11 If you have a dress form, place T-shirt on form. Pin pleats to chalk marks made in steps 1 and 2. Overlap pleats 1 in. (2.5cm) at center back. Or, try on top and have a friend (carefully!) pin pleats to T-shirt. Take care T-shirt is not pulled taut while it is being pinned.

Step 12 Hand-sew pleats to T-shirt, removing pins as you stitch.

Doily Racer-Back Tank

Everyone is so concerned with making a dramatic entrance, but what about an attention-grabbing exit? This standard racer-back tank turns truly spectacular at the reverse with the addition of hand-dyed doilies and a smattering of sequins.

Materials

Fabric dye in plum or desired color

Large bucket

Protective gloves

Chopstick or paint stirrer

Paper towels (optional)

One large round doily 12-in. dia. (30.1cm)

One medium round doily 6-in. dia (15.5cm)

Ten small round doilies 3-in. dia (7.6cm)

Racer-back tank

Straight pins

Hand-sewing needle

Matching sewing thread

Fabric scissors

Assorted sequins (optional)

Dyeing to meet you

Doily sizes for this project are not set in stone. Any size, number, and even shape of doily can be used.

You can use vintage doilies for this project because when you dye them, any stains will be nicely covered!

If you can't find suitable vintage doilies in a thrift store or flea market, check your local craft store. It may seem an unlikely place to find premade crocheted doilies, but they are used for all kinds of crafts and are surprisingly inexpensive and available in lots of sizes.

You could also try cutting out shapes from heavy lace for a similar effect, but you will almost certainly have to treat the edges to prevent them from fraying.

Remember, dye is designed to change the color permanently! Make sure you don't get any splashes of it on yourself, your clothes, or on any surrounding household furnishings. If you dye your items in a washing machine, run it through one or two washing cycles without clothes afterwards to be absolutely certain that there is no dye left in the machine.

Step 1 Following manufacturer's directions, make dye bath in bucket. Wear protective gloves and cover your clothing and work area. (See "Dyeing fabric" on page 63.)

Step 2 Wet doilies with clean water, then add to dye bath. Leave them to soak following manufacturer's directions, stirring every few minutes using chopstick or paint stirrer.

Step 3 When you feel the color is the depth you desire, rinse doilies under cool running water until water runs clear. Squeeze excess water from doilies without wringing them, and gently form them back into their original shape. Hang doilies to dry or place them on paper towels.

Step 4 Find center back of racer-back tank, and pin large doily to tank.

Step 5 With their edges touching, pin medium doily centered above large doily. Make sure medium doily is half on fabric of tank and half on straps.

Step 6 Using whipstitch, hand-sew large doily to tank and to medium doily. (See photo of whipstitch on page 23.) Sew medium doily to tank fabric. Do not sew to straps.

Step 7 With their edges touching, pin small doilies to either side of medium doily and centered over straps. Do not pin doilies to straps. Pin edge of last small doily on either side to front of tank. Length of doily straps should be same as original tank straps.

Step 8 Whipstitch edges of doilies together, being careful not to sew them to straps.

Step 9 Neatly cut off original tank straps. Whipstitch last small doilies of strap to front of tank.

Step 10 You may choose to sew sequins scattered randomly either all over your tank or just on doilies as shown. (See "Sequins" on page 55.)

Romance Skirt

Every girl needs that perfect, swishy skirt that makes her feel like she's the star of one of those arty French films—this is that skirt. It's perfect for strolling along the Seine in the late afternoon or making your office party a little more chic.

Materials

1 yd. (.91m) fusible webbing
1 yd. (.91m) sheer fabric with a large floral print
Iron
Fabric scissors
Full skirt in taffeta
Pressing cloth
Sewing machine
Matching and contrasting sewing threads
Hand-sewing needle
Sequins in various colors

Flower power

You could also cut out some of the larger motifs from a floral printed non-sheer fabric to make this skirt. Just make sure the fabric is light enough in weight so that the taffeta skirt can support the motifs.

An alternative idea is to use some small lace doilies or crochet motifs, as described in the "Doily Racer-Back Tank" on page 85.

Step 1 Peel off paper from one side of fusible webbing. Place sheer fabric over it, right side up. Iron fabric so that it adheres to webbing with no puckers.

Step 2 Cut out several motifs in different sizes from fused fabric to make appliqués.

Step 3 Peel off other side of paper backing from appliqués. Arrange appliqués on skirt as desired. Set your iron to a temperature that matches the fabric of your skirt and appliqués. Place a pressing cloth over appliqués when fusing so fabric isn't damaged.

Step 4 Machine-sew, using straight stitch and matching thread, along edge of all appliqués. For added interest, stitch in random patterns within appliqués as well.

Step 5 Using contrasting thread, sew around bottom of skirt in a random wavy, meandering line, running straight in a few places if you like. You can also sew around waistband if skirt has one.

Step 6 Sew sequins to skirt in a random pattern of meandering lines. (See "Sequins" on page 55.)

Prize Ribbon Skirt

I love the look of bright grosgrain ribbons against a nubby tweed. This look always wins high marks in my book. You can place a ribbon panel down the front as shown on page 92 or place a ribbon stripe all around your skirt. The prize ribbon shown at the waist of the skirt is made with a pinback so you can wear your skirt with or without it.

Materials

For the skirt:

Tape measure

High-waisted skirt in tweed

1 yd. (.91m) each of grosgrain ribbons in various widths and colors

Fabric scissors

Fabric adhesive

Sewing machine

Matching sewing thread

For the prize ribbon:

1 yd. (.91m) of 1-in. wide (25mm) wide grosgrain ribbon

Straight pins

Hand-sewing needle

Matching sewing thread

Small lengths of ribbon from skirt

Jewelry adhesive

$\frac{1}{2}$-in. dia. (13mm) brass charm

1-in. dia. (25mm) button in contrasting color

$1\frac{1}{2}$-in. long (3.8cm) pinback

Step 1 Measure length of your skirt. Cut each ribbon to that length plus an extra $1\frac{1}{2}$ in. (3.8cm) for turning under ends.

Step 2 Place skirt with front side face up. Determine where ribbons will be positioned. Have each ribbon extend $\frac{3}{4}$ in. (19mm) beyond waistband and hem. Measure to be sure ribbons are parallel with each other and with side seam of skirt. Use dots of fabric adhesive to glue ribbons to skirt. Turn top and bottom ends of ribbon onto wrong side of waistband and hem, and adhere. I chose to use ribbons as a center panel but you can add them anywhere to the skirt.

Step 3 Finish by machine-topstitching on both sides of all ribbons. I like a slightly off-kilter stitch because it makes the rather preppy ribbons look a little less precious, but if you are a perfectionist, sew precisely $\frac{1}{16}$ in. (2mm) from edge of ribbon.

Making the prize ribbon

Step 1 Fold one end of 1-in. wide (2.5cm) ribbon under ¼ in. (6mm), and pin.

Step 2 Make a slightly angled ¼ in. (6mm) fold every ½ in. (13mm) on right side of ribbon. Pin each fold.

Step 3 Fold other end of ribbon under ¼ in. (6mm), and pin.

Step 4 Machine-stitch close to pinned edge of ribbon, removing pins as you sew.

Step 5 Starting at center, coil ribbon into a spiral. Pin to secure and hand-sew layers together.

Step 6 Cut six pieces of ribbon left from skirt. Fan them out slightly to look like ribbons hanging from a prize ribbon as shown in photograph. Hand-sew together at unfanned end. Hand-sew unfanned end to back of prize ribbon.

Step 7 Hand-sew button to center of prize ribbon. Use jewelry adhesive to glue charm to center of button.

Step 8 Hand-sew pinback to back of prize ribbon, 1 in. (2.5cm) above center.

Step 9 Pin prize ribbon to skirt wherever you like.

Rainy Day Skirt

I got the idea for this skirt while I was strolling through my local thrift store where plaid wool skirts abound. Appliqués are a quick and fun way to breathe new life into this old stand-by. I love mixing patterns with colors that complement the colors in the weave of the tweed. You can wear this skirt in any weather, but I guarantee it will brighten up a rainy day.

Materials

Black fine-tip permanent marker
Fusible webbing
Paper scissors
Fabric scraps in three different patterns
Fabric scissors
A-line skirt in plaid
Iron
Embroidery hoop
Size 7 embroidery/crewel needle
Embroidery floss in colors as desired
Embroidery scissors

Step 1 Use marker to trace one small cloud and two large clouds on page 172 onto paper side of fusible web. Use a photocopier to enlarge or reduce clouds before tracing if desired.

Step 2 Cut out clouds leaving 1-in. (2.5cm) border on all sides. Following manufacturer's directions, fuse webbing to wrong side of fabrics. Cut out cloud appliqués. (See "Appliqué" on page 56.)

Step 3 Peel off paper backing, and arrange appliqués on skirt. Press each cloud with iron following manufacturer's instructions.

Step 4 Using four strands of floss in needle, embroider split stitch around each cloud. Embroider over fabric edge to prevent it from fraying. (See "Split stitch" on page 30.)

Step 5 Using six strands of floss in needle, embroider running stitches in various colors below clouds to indicate rain. (See "Running stitch" on page 20.)

Garden Vine Shrug

I learned how to needle-felt a year ago and I've been hooked ever since! It's such an easy way to transform dull sweaters into something beautiful. Once you get the technique down, you can adorn your wardrobe with any design your heart desires. Make sure your sweater is 100 percent wool or the design won't felt successfully! The petals and leaves on this shrug are felted separately, so secure them with small stitches on the reverse side.

Materials

Chalk-backed dressmaker's paper

Pencil

Shrug in wool

Green, blue, and purple wool roving

Small amounts of hot pink, and yellow wool roving

Needle-felting tool

Needle-felting mat

Hand-sewing needle

Matching sewing thread

Green fingers

Don't have any wool roving? You can also cut design pieces from wool felt scraps and needle-felt the pieces onto the shrug.

❖

This design would also look pretty applied to a wool scarf or a sweater coat.

❖

Remember, your garment needs to be 100 percent wool. Felting does not work well on synthetic yarns.

❖

If you are using a light-colored garment, as I have done here, check that the roving or felt you are using is colorfast. You don't want your hard work ruined in the first wash. Soak bits of each color of roving or felt in cold water. Place them on a white paper towel. If any color bleeds onto the towel, the roving or felt is not colorfast and the garment should be dry cleaned.

❖

Even if you are doing a tiny detail, always place the area being felted on the felting mat. Never hold the work in your hands when using the needle-felting tool. Felting needles are very sharp!

Step 1 Enlarge design on page 170 to 125 percent. Make two copies, one a reverse (or mirror image). You can alter design as needed to fit garment you are needle-felting, but make changes before you transfer design.

Step 2 Sandwich transfer paper between photocopy of design and front of shrug. Go over all lines of design using pencil to transfer it to shrug. (See "Transferring with chalk-backed dressmaker's paper" on page 30.)

Step 3 To make vine, pull a long strand of green roving, and roll it into a strand. Place on shrug following design line. (See "Needle Felting" on page 47.)

Step 4 Place felting mat under shrug, and punch strand of roving using needle-felting tool. Continue punching, moving mat as you work, until vine is completed.

Step 5 To make petals, pull a small piece of blue roving, twist it slightly, and double it over into a petal shape. Place on mat and punch using needle-felting tool until petal shape is flat and roving is bound together.

Step 6 To add purple detail, repeat technique in step 5 using a slightly smaller piece of roving. Punch purple petal into blue petal. For each flower, make one large petal and two small petals.

Step 7 Follow step 5 and make leaves using green roving.

Step 8 Place petals and leaves on shrug where indicated by transferred design.

Step 9 Place mat under shrug, and punch each piece using needle-felting tool.

Step 10 To make dots, roll small pieces of hot-pink and yellow roving into balls, and punch them into shrug using needle-felting tool. Alter size of dots as desired.

Step 11 To further secure petals and leaves, use needle and thread to make small stitches on wrong side of shrug.

Tulips and Tweed Jacket

Freezer paper was certainly not invented for making stencils—but it may as well have been because it is absolutely perfect for this technique! All you have to do is iron the freezer-paper stencil onto the garment you want to adorn and stencil away. This little tweed jacket looks great with a few strategically placed blooms in a shade of pink that really pops.

Materials

Chalk-backed dressmaker's paper
Pencil
Freezer paper
Cutting mat
Craft knife
Iron
Jacket in plaid
Small sponge brush
Fabric ink in pink or as desired
Pressing cloth
Assorted sequins (optional)
Hand-sewing needle (optional)
Matching sewing thread (optional)

Step 1 Enlarge designs on page 170 to 110 percent. Transfer or simply trace design onto matte side of freezer paper. (See "Transferring with chalk-backed dressmaker's paper" on page 30.)

Step 2 Working on cutting mat, cut out stencils using craft knife. (See "Freezer-paper stencils" on page 60.)

Step 3 With shiny side of freezer paper face down, iron large stencil onto right front of jacket. Make sure stencil adheres completely.

Step 4 Dip sponge brush in ink, and dab ink onto stencil. Don't brush on the ink or it will run under edges of stencil.

Step 5 Carefully peel off stencil. Let stenciled design dry completely.

Step 6 Repeat steps 3 – 5 with small stencil on left front of jacket.

Step 7 Following manufacturer's directions, heat-set designs with iron, covering design areas with press cloth.

Step 8 If you choose, hand-sew some sequins to parts of design for added texture and sparkle. (See "Sequins" on page 55.)

Stencil style

To prevent jacket from shifting while you work, pin or tape it securely to your work surface.

If you are stenciling onto a lightweight fabric, such as a T-shirt, place a piece of cardboard between the front and the back of the garment to prevent the ink from bleeding through.

Enid Shift

This sweet bejeweled shift dress reminds me of the decorations on the whimsical 1960s bags by Enid Collins. Flat-back jewels really pack a punch, so I like to limit the palette to two or three colors. You can follow the pattern here or create your own.

Materials

Plain shift dress with yoke
Selection of large, medium, and small flat-back
    jewels with sewing holes
Digital camera or pencil and paper
Jewelry adhesive for fabric
Hand-sewing needle
Matching sewing thread

Step 1 Lay out jewels in desired pattern on yoke of dress. Take a picture or draw design so you have it for reference.

Step 2 Glue each jewel in position with jewelry adhesive, being careful not to get adhesive on fabric around each jewel. (See "Flat-back Jewels" on page 53.)

Step 3 Double knot thread in needle, and beginning on wrong side of dress, sew through each jewel hole twice. End thread with knot on wrong side of dress, and cut thread end. Repeat for each hole.

Glitz and glam

You can achieve a similar design by sewing buttons or beads onto the yoke of a shift dress. Follow the same technique used for the flat-back jewels.

The pattern of jewels on this shift is symmetrical. You could also create an asymmetrical design. Just arrange the jewels needed to complete your design on the dress before you begin securing them to the fabric. This way you can adjust the elements until you are totally happy with the effect.

Studded Blouse

Think of this top as your "go-to" for going out. The edginess of the studs is a perfect foil for the sensuous drape of the satin. Studs would look equally fabulous on a pencil skirt or a favorite pair of jeans. They are surprisingly easy to set and don't require expensive tools.

Materials

Satin blouse with waistband
Several packs of studs in different sizes, shapes, and colors
Ruler
Water-soluble fabric pen
Needle-nose pliers

Step 1 To determine how many rows of studs you need for your waistband, lay out studs in one column. Measure, and then mark rows on inside of blouse using a water-soluble pen.

Step 2 Working row by row, push studs through blouse fabric. Use needle-nose pliers to bend prongs at a 90-deg. angle to stud. (See "Studs" on page 54.)

Step 3 Curve point of each prong so that it is inserted into fabric at center of stud.

Step 4 You may also choose to add a few studs in a random design to blouse ties.

Sparkle and shine

You can use studs to create a pattern on the bodice of the blouse as well. Mark the pattern using water-soluble ink, then apply the studs following your design.

This project would also look great substituting flat-back jewels. For these, follow the techniques described in "Enid Shift" on page 102.

Deco Sweater

Bias tape is usually used in garment construction, but it also looks great as an embellishment. Because the fabric for bias tape is cut on a diagonal, it is easily manipulated into curved designs. You can make your own bias tape from any of the endless variety of fabrics available to create a look that reflects your own unique taste.

Materials

Pullover sweater in wool

Water-soluble pen

Measuring tape

½ yd. (.46m) each of two cotton prints that coordinate or contrast with sweater

Rotary cutter, straight edge, and cutting mat

½-in. (13mm) bias-tape maker

Iron

Straight pins

Hand-sewing needle

Matching sewing thread

Step 1 Use water-soluble pen to draw design for bias tape on sweater referring to layout diagram on page 174.

Step 2 Measure length of bias-tape strip needed to cover lines you have just drawn. Add 1 in. (2.5cm) to each measurement.

Step 3 Working on cutting mat, prepare fabric for bias cutting. (See "Bias tape" on page 44.) Use rotary cutter and straight edge to cut 1-in. wide (2.5cm) strips of fabric in two colors. Cut as many strips as you need to equal length determined in step 2. Sew strips together to achieve length.

Step 4 Cut one end of each strip on an angle to make it easier to insert end into bias-tape maker. Feed strips through bias-tape maker, ironing tape as you work. Fold each strip in half to make double-fold tape, and iron.

Step 5 Pin strips of bias tape to sweater over design lines. Fold under tape ends, and pin.

Step 6 Slipstitch both edges of each strip to sweater, removing pins as you work. (See "Slipstitch" on page 20.)

Vivienne Vest

I love argyle patterns, but sometimes they can be a bit, well, stuffy. With its frayed edges and yarn embroidery, this vest is more punk rock than prep school, à la Vivienne Westwood, one of my favorite designers. If you don't like vests, this pattern can easily be adapted to a skirt, a dress, or even a tote bag.

Materials

Chalk-backed dressmaker's paper

Pencil

Lightweight cardboard

Paper scissors

Tailor's chalk

Old plaid wool skirt or ¼ yd. (.23m) plaid wool fabric

Vest in wool or synthetic knit

Fusible webbing

Iron

Sewing machine

Matching sewing thread

Worsted-weight yarn in three colors

Size 18 chenille needle

Step 1 Enlarge diamond pattern on page 171 to 250 percent or desired size. Use dressmaker's paper to transfer diamond onto cardboard. Cut out template. (See "Transferring with chalk-backed dressmaker's paper" on page 30.)

Step 2 Trace around template using tailor's chalk onto plaid wool. Make sure that fabric weave is parallel with edges of diamond. Cut out three diamonds. Then fray ¾ in. (19mm) fringe on all edges.

Step 3 Mark a line down center of vest using tailor's chalk.

Step 4 Cut fusible webbing for each diamond. Remove paper from one side of webbing. Following manufacturer's directions, use iron to fuse webbing to wrong side of each diamond. (See "Appliqué" on page 56.)

Step 5 Remove paper from webbing. Place top diamond on vest approximately 2 in. (5.1cm) below neckline. Have points of diamond on chalk line. Use iron to fuse diamond to vest. Fuse middle and bottom diamonds to vest along chalk line, making sure points of diamonds touch slightly.

Step 6 Using straight stitch, machine-sew diamonds to vest ¾ in. (19mm) from all edges.

Step 7 Referring to photograph, use chalk to draw stitching lines for embroidered diamonds. Use running stitch and yarn to embroider fabric diamonds along stitching lines and chalk-marked diamonds. An embroidery hoop isn't necessary. (See "Running stitch" on page 20.)

Daisy Sundress

This little dress has comfy, roomy pockets perfect for holding sweets or just stashing necessities. You could embellish several dresses with different fabrics, one for every day of the week. You might not want to wear anything else!

Materials

Chalk-backed dressmaker's paper

Pencil

Lightweight cardboard

Paper scissors

Water-soluble pen

¼ yd. (22.9cm) each of two cotton prints

¼ yd. (22.9cm) of solid cotton (for pocket lining)

¼ yd. (22.9cm) of lightweight iron-on interfacing

Fabric scissors

Straight pins

Sewing machine

Matching sewing thread

Chopstick or other pointed tool

Simple dress or jumper in knit fabric

Seam ripper

Rotary cutter, straight edge, and cutting mat

Iron

Dress form (optional)

Hand-sewing needle

Four buttons 1-in. (25mm) dia.

Step 1 Enlarge pocket on page 171 to 160 percent. Use dressmaker's paper to transfer pocket onto cardboard. Cut out template using paper scissors. (See "Transferring with chalk-backed dressmaker's paper" on page 30.)

Step 2 Use water-soluble pen to trace template twice each on one of the cotton prints, lining fabric, and interfacing. Cut out pieces using fabric scissors.

Step 3 For each pocket, press interfacing to wrong side of lining. With right sides facing, pin cotton print to lining.

Step 4 Sew together using ½ in. (13mm) seam allowance. Leave 3 in. (7.6cm) unsewn for turning. (See "Tips" on page 23.) Trim seam allowance to within ³⁄₁₆ in. (5mm) of seam. Clip curves and across corners. (See "Tips" on page 21.)

Step 5 Turn right side out, pushing corners out with chopstick. Fold raw edges of opening to inside, and pin.

Step 6 Sew pinned opening closed using slipstitch, and iron. (See "Slipstitch" on page 20.)

Step 7 Machine-topstitch ⅛ in. (3mm) from edge on all sides, if desired. Set pockets aside.

Step 8 Use seam ripper to carefully remove straps from dress.

Step 9 Measure straps. Multiply width by two, and add 1 in. (2.5cm). Add 2 in. (5.1cm) to length.

Step 10 Working on cutting mat, use rotary cutter and straight edge to cut two strips from second cotton print, and two strips from interfacing. Iron interfacing to wrong side of cotton print.

Step 11 For each strip, fold strip in half with wrong sides together, and iron. Fold both long edges of strip ½ in. (13mm) to inside. Pin and iron.

Step 12 Topstitch ⅛ in. (3mm) in from both edges of both straps.

Step 13 If possible, place dress on dress form or place on flat surface. Pin straps to front and back of dress in same location as original straps.

Step 14 Pin pockets to sides of dress, where desired.

Step 15 Slipstitch pockets and straps to dress. (See "Slipstitch" on page 20.)

Step 16 Referring to photograph on page 111, sew buttons to dress.

Ribbon Rose Tunic

Ribbon embroidery is dainty, romantic, and lends a wonderful dimensional quality to flowers that can't be achieved with traditional embroidery. These roses look perfect scattered across the top of a summery cotton tunic. Because it makes a pretty large impact, use ribbon embroidery sparingly, or you will begin to look like a wedding cake!

Materials

Chalk-backed dressmaker's paper
Pencil
Plain tunic in lightweight cotton
3 yards (2.7m) 4mm-wide silk ribbon each in
    peach, apricot, light green, and medium green
Hand-sewing needle
Matching sewing thread
Straight pins (optional)
Tear-away stabilizer (optional)
Size 26 chenille needle
Embroidery hoop
Embroidery scissors

Step 1 Enlarge pattern on page 173 to desired size. Transfer design to the front of tunic using dressmaker's paper. (See "Transferring with chalk-backed dressmaker's paper" on page 30.)

Step 2 Make seven folded ribbon roses using apricot and peach ribbons. Thread a hand-sewing needle with sewing thread to match color of ribbon; knot end; and set aside.

Step 3 For each rose, cut a 12-in. length (30.5cm) of ribbon. Fold 1 in. (2.5cm) of one end of ribbon toward you on a 45-deg. angle. (See "Folded ribbon roses" on page 36.)

Step 4 Roll diagonal fold onto longer end of ribbon five times to form center of rose. Sew through bottom edges of rose center to secure layers.

Step 5 Fold longer end of ribbon away from you and on a 45-deg. angle. Roll rose center onto fold. Sew bottom edge to secure.

Step 6 Repeat folding ribbon, rolling rose onto fold, and stitching. At the same time, roll the rose slightly higher each time to give it depth. Be sure to roll loosely.

Step 7 When rose is about ½ in. (13mm), trim ends to ½ in. (13mm); tuck under rose; and tack to secure.

Step 8 If tunic is made of very lightweight fabric, you may want to pin tear-away stabilizer to wrong side of fabric, behind embroidery, to reinforce the area and better support the flowers.

Step 9 Place tunic in embroidery hoop. Depending on the size of hoop, you may need to reposition it as you embroider leaves and stems.

Step 10 Using medium-green ribbon, embroider stems by making lines of twisted ribbon stitches. (See "A stitch in time" on page 34 for securing ribbon in needle, and "Twisted ribbon stitch" on page 33.)

Step 11 For all ribbon embroidery, fasten ribbon ends on wrong side of blouse with hand-sewing needle and matching sewing thread.

Step 12 Using light-green ribbon, work ribbon stitch for leaves. (See "Ribbon stitch" on page 33.)

Step 13 Sew ribbon roses to tunic, making sure to hide stitching under flowers.

Step 14 Tear away excess stabilizer on wrong side of fabric.

Little Birdie Mini

Appliqué gets a makeover in reverse! If you don't want to use denim for the reverse-appliqué fabric, substitute another heavyweight fabric. This little birdie would also look sweet on a denim jacket or even on the back pocket of a pair of jeans.

Materials

Chalk-backed dressmaker's paper
Pencil
Mini skirt in denim
Straight pins
8-in. (20cm) square of denim in a color that
    contrasts with mini skirt
Fabric scissors
Embroidery hoop
Size 7 embroidery/crewel needle
Embroidery floss in color to match stitching
    on skirt
Embroidery scissors

Step 1 Enlarge bird silhouette on page 172 by 125 percent, and transfer design onto skirt where desired. (See "Transferring with chalk-backed dressmaker's paper" on page 30.)

Step 2 Pin denim square on inside of skirt, making sure it is centered under bird outline.

Step 3 Place outline area in embroidery hoop. With four strands of floss in needle, backstitch bird outline. (See "Backstitch" on page 31.)

Step 4 Carefully cut out bird silhouette about $\frac{1}{16}$ in. (2mm) from stitching to reveal darker denim underneath.

Step 5 Remove pins, and trim off excess denim fabric inside skirt.

Accessories

Even the simplest of outfits becomes fashion forward when
paired with the perfect accessory. Keep up with trends
or sport your own personal style by giving your accessories
a facelift using these fresh embellishing techniques.

Ribbon-Wrapped Bangles and Hoops

Have you ever been getting ready to go out, but just can't find that perfect bangle or hoop earrings to go with your otherwise stunning outfit? Well, never fear, you can make these accessories in about ten minutes, customizing them to match any outfit in your wardrobe. Grosgrain, silk, brocade, and velvet ribbons all look equally gorgeous when wrapped around a bangle or a simple pair of hoop earrings.

Materials

Plastic or wood bangle or pair of hoop earrings
Approximately 2 yds. (1.8m) ribbon for each
bangle or one pair of hoops (Note: length of
ribbon needed depends on ribbon width.
Wide ribbon requires fewer wraps than
narrow ribbon.)
Hot-glue gun and glue sticks

Step 1 Apply a dot of hot glue to inside of bangle (or hoop). Press ribbon end into glue at a slight angle to bangle.

Step 2 Tightly wrap ribbon around bangle, adding dots of hot glue to inside of bangle every few wraps. Make sure ribbon lays flat on surface of bangle as you wrap.

Step 3 To finish, dot inside with hot glue, and adhere end of ribbon on inside.

All wrapped up

For a variation, wrap strips of fabric around the bangles or hoops. You can either cut neat strips using a rotary cutter, straight edge, and cutting mat, or you can tear them for a rougher look. Cotton, silk, and sheer fabrics are all great options and come in interesting patterns and textures.

Patchwork Pocket Tote

Everyone needs a tote bag or two. This one's just great for groceries, library books, or even a day at the beach. Patchwork may seem a little old-fashioned at first, but once you get the hang of making a patchwork square, you will find that the stylistic possibilities are endless.

Materials

Plain canvas tote

Seam ripper

Tape measure

Rotary cutter, straight edge, and cutting mat

¼ yard (22.9cm) each of five cotton prints

Iron

Straight pins

Sewing machine

Matching and contrasting sewing threads

Fabric scissors

Water-soluble pen

¼ yd. (.23m) medium-weight iron-on interfacing

¼ yd. (.23m) solid cotton for lining

Chopstick or other pointed tool

Hand-sewing needle

Heavy-duty hand-sewing needle (size 7 sharps)

Embroidery scissors

Step 1 Using a seam ripper, remove canvas straps from tote. Measure straps. Multiply width by two, and add 1 in. (2.5cm). Add 2 in. (5.1cm) to length. Working on cutting mat, use rotary cutter and straight edge to cut two strips from two of the print fabrics.

Step 2 For each strap, iron one long edge of strip ½ in. (13mm) to wrong side. Place canvas strap on wrong side of strip, with one long edge inside pressed edge of strip. Center canvas strap from top to bottom of strip. Fold other long edge of strip over canvas strap, encasing it, and iron. Turn long raw edge under, pin, and iron.

Step 3 Machine-topstitch both long edges ¼ in. (6mm) from edge, removing pins as you sew.

Step 4 Work on cutting mat using rotary cutter and straight edge. From cotton prints, cut four pieces each in the following sizes:

A = 1 in. × 2 in. (2.5cm x 5.1cm)
B = 1 in. × 4 in. (2.5cm x 11.4cm)
C = 2 in. × 5½ in. (5.1cm x 14.0cm)
D = 3 in. × 3½ in. (7.6cm x 8.9cm)
E = 3 in. × 2½ in. (7.6cm x 6.4cm)

Step 5 Use ¼ in. (6mm) seam allowance when assembling blocks. Pin seams before sewing as needed. Iron seams as you work, pressing toward darkest fabric. Refer to block diagram below to assemble one block. Make four blocks.

Step 6 Sew **A** to **B**. Sew **A/B** to **C**. Sew **D** to **E**. Sew **D/E** to **C**.

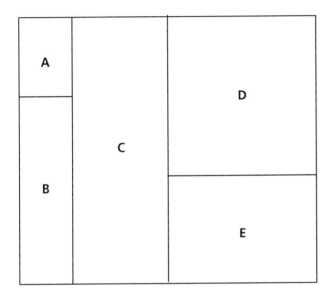

Step 7 Sew four blocks together, arranging blocks to match photograph or as desired. Iron seams.

Step 8 Fold patchwork in half, and use fabric scissors to trim two rounded corners in both thicknesses.

Step 9 Using patchwork as template, trace same shape on interfacing and wrong side of lining fabric with water-soluble pen. Cut out pieces.

Step 10 Iron interfacing on wrong side of lining. With right sides facing, pin patchwork to lining. Sew together using ½-in. (13mm) seam allowance. Leave 3 in. (7.6cm) unsewn for turning. (See "Tips" on page 23.) Trim seam allowance to within ³⁄₁₆ in. (5mm) of seam. Clip curves and across corners. (See "Tips" on page 21.)

Step 11 Turn right side out, pushing corners out with chopstick. Fold raw edges of opening to inside, and pin. Sew opening closed, using slipstitch, and iron. (See "Slipstitch" on page 20.)

Step 12 Pin pocket to center outside of tote. Slipstitch pocket to tote using hand-sewing needle.

Step 13 Pin handles to inside of tote. Turn under ends 1 in. (2.5cm).

Step 14 Thread size 3 needle with two strands of contrasting thread. To secure straps, sew 1 in. (2.5cm) square of stitching through all layers. Then sew an "X" in the center of each stitched square.

Bits and pieces

This tote has a patchwork pocket on only one side, but you could make pockets for both sides to double the carrying capacity!

The patchwork in this project is a simple design of asymmetric blocks, but you could use any quilt-block design for this project. Browse through a few quilting books to see if anything catches your eye.

If you only want a patchwork appliqué on your tote, omit the interfacing and lining, and stitch your patchwork block to one side of the tote. Turn the edges of block ½ in. (13mm) to wrong side, and iron. Pin; then hand-sew to outside of tote using slipstitch. (See "Slipstitch" on page 20.)

Bits and Pieces Scarf

A few years ago, I bought a gigantic box of doilies at a yard sale (score!) and I have been incorporating them into many of my craft projects ever since. There are so many fantastic doilies out there, mostly made with immense care and attention to detail. Instead of tucking them into boxes and storing them in the attic, use them to make beautiful things that incorporate the vintage with the new!

Materials

Tear-away stabilizer, 10 in. (25.4cm)
    wide x desired length
15 to 20 doilies in different shapes and sizes
    (Note: when purchasing, lay out your choices
    in shape of scarf to make certain you buy
    enough.)
Digital camera (optional)
Paper (optional)
Pencil (optional)
Fabric dye in rose or desired color
Fabric dye in red or desired color
Large bucket
Protective gloves
Chopstick or paint stirrer
Paper towels (optional)
Straight pins
Sewing machine
Sewing thread in matching or contrasting color,
    as desired

Step 1 Place length of stabilizer on a large surface. Arrange doilies on stabilizer. Doilies should slightly overlap each other. If desired, use a rectangular doily at one end of scarf.

Step 2 Take a photo of arrangement or make a simple sketch so that you have a record of the design to refer to when assembling.

Step 3 Decide which doilies you want to dye. Dyed ones should be scattered randomly throughout the design.

Step 4 Following manufacturer's directions, make rose dye bath in bucket. Wear protective gloves, and cover your clothing and work area. (See "Dyeing fabric" on page 63.)

Step 5 Wet doilies with clean water, then add to dye bath. Let them soak, following manufacturer's directions, stirring every few minutes using a chopstick or paint stirrer.

Step 6 When you feel the color is the shade you desire, rinse the doilies under cool running water until water runs clear. You can take the doilies out of the dye bath at different times to get varying shades of color.

Step 7 Squeeze excess water from doilies without wringing them, and gently pull them back into their original shape. Hang doilies to dry, or place them on paper towels.

Step 8 Repeat steps 4 – 7, using red dye and other doilies.

Step 9 Referring to your photograph or sketch, place dry doilies on length of stabilizer. Pin to stabilizer and to each other where they overlap.

Step 10 Use medium-length straight stitch to machine-sew around each doily, removing pins as you sew.

Step 11 Tear away stabilizer from doilies.

Waste not, want not

When you are purchasing vintage doilies, it doesn't matter if they have a few light, minor stains because they will be concealed by the dye. If in doubt, wash the doilies before dyeing, and use a prewash stain-removing product.

Avoid any doilies that are torn or have holes, unless you can work around them in your project. It's not easy to repair the lacy stitches unless you are an expert!

This project will be most successful if the doilies are made of threads of a similar weight, but don't worry about having lots of different designs. The more interesting the details, the better!

Don't dye all the doilies. It's nice to leave a few in their natural vintage state for that authentic "shabby-chic" look.

Embossed Velvet Capelet

Embossing velvet is the process of using heat to press patterns into the pile of velvet fabric. It seems like it ought to be impossible to do this at home, but the technique is fairly simple. You could also experiment embossing designs into velvet using rubber stamps. Here, a simple capelet is embossed to create a sophisticated garment for a dressy night out.

Materials

Assorted pieces of heavy lace, crochet motifs, and doilies
Plain capelet in rayon velvet
Digital camera (optional)
Pencil (optional)
Paper (optional)
Spray bottle with water
Iron

Step 1 Place pieces of lace, doilies, and crochet motifs on capelet in pleasing arrangement. Don't overlap the pieces and don't use too many in one area, or the design may end up too fussy. Move things around until you are happy with the overall effect.

Step 2 Take a picture of the design for reference, or make a simple sketch.

Step 3 Place embossing motif to be stamped on work surface. Place capelet, with wrong side of fabric face up, over motif.

Step 4 Use spray bottle to *lightly* mist wrong side of fabric over area of motif.

Step 5 Hold a dry iron, set on "rayon," over fabric for ten seconds without moving it. Do not iron back and forth. This will cause the image to be blurry. Change position of iron, and iron again for another ten seconds. The embossed design will appear on wrong side of fabric. (See "Embossing on Velvet" on page 62.)

Step 6 Continue positioning and embossing motifs until you have completed your design.

Step 7 Hang the capelet to prevent wrinkles. Do not iron over the motifs again as the embossing may become blurry.

Boldly go

Embossed-velvet garments and accessories should be dry-cleaned to preserve the embossing.

If you don't love the look of lace, you can use rubber stamps for embossing.

Remember to choose bold, simple designs for best results. Closely spaced, delicate details will emboss as a solid shape.

Before embossing, hold an iron over a small inconspicuous part on the wrong side of the velvet for ten seconds to make certain that the temperature of the iron is not too hot, which will melt the fiber.

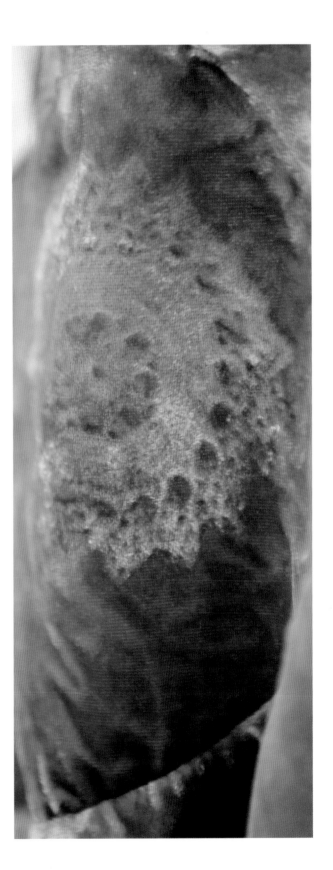

Sakura Blossom Headband

A simple fabric headband becomes a confection fit for a fairy tale with the addition of crocheted flowers. I liked the idea that these flowers would dramatically frame the face, so I sewed some of them on the edge of the headband. If you are completely baffled by crochet (or just short on time), you can buy crocheted flowers at a fabric store or vintage shop.

Materials

For the small flower:
2 yds. (1.8m) sportweight cotton yarn
Size D/3 (3.25mm) crochet hook

For the medium flower and the layered flowers:
5 yds. (4.6m) DK weight cotton yarn in color A
5 yds. (4.6m) DK weight cotton yarn in color B
Size E/4 (3.50mm) crochet hook
Size 16 tapestry needle

For blocking:
Straight pins
Blocking board or padded surface at least ¼-in. thick (6mm)
Spray bottle of water

For finishing:
Fabric-covered headband
Fabric scissors
Hand-sewing needle
Matching sewing thread

Crochet abbreviations

ch = chain stitch
ch-sp = chain space
dc = double crochet
hdc = half double crochet
() = Work the directions contained inside the parentheses into the stitch indicated.
sc = single crochet
sl st = slip stitch
tr = treble (triple) crochet
* = repeat instructions following the single asterisk as directed.
RS = right side, right sides

Small flower

Step 1 Make a slip knot, leaving a 5-in. (12.7cm) tail and place on crochet hook.

Step 2 Ch 4. Join ch with a sl st forming a ring.

Step 3 Round 1 (RS) *Ch 4, sl st into ring; repeat from * around 4 more times more, working over the tail—5 ch-4 loops. Pull the tail to close center of flower. Thread tail in tapestry needle; then weave in tail on the wrong side.

Step 4 Round 2 *In next ch-4 loop, work (sl st, ch 2, 3 dc, ch 2, sl st); repeat from * around 4 times more--5 petals made. Cut yarn leaving a 5-in. (12.7cm) tail. Fasten off. Weave in tail on the wrong side.

Medium solid-color flower

Step 1 Make a slip knot, leaving a 5-in. (12.7cm) tail and place on crochet hook.

Step 2 Ch 6. Join ch with a sl st, forming a ring.

Step 3 Round 1 (RS) *Ch 4, sc in ring; repeat from * around 4 times more working over the tail—5 ch-4 loops. Pull the tail to close center of flower. Thread tail in tapestry needle; then weave in tail on the wrong side.

Step 4 Round 2 *In next ch-4 loop work (sc, hdc, 4 dc, hdc, sc); repeat from * around 4 times more—5 petals made. Cut yarn leaving a 5-in. (12.7cm) tail. Fasten off. Weave in tail on the wrong side.

Two-color layered flower

Step 1 For top layer, use color A to make a slip knot, leaving a 5-in. (12.7cm) tail, and place on crochet hook.

Step 2 Ch 4. Join ch with a sl st forming a ring.

Step 3 Round 1 (RS) *Ch 4, sl st in ring; repeat from * around 4 times more working over the tail—5 ch-4 loops. Pull the tail to close center of flower. Thread tail in tapestry needle; then weave in tail on the wrong side.

Step 4 Round 2 *In next ch-4 loop work (sl st, ch 2, 3 dc, ch 2, sl st); repeat from * around 4 times more--5 petals made.

Step 5 Working behind the petals of the flower just made, insert the hook through the next space created by the ch-4 loop of Round 1 and sc over the foundation ring; working in the same manner, *ch 5, sc into the foundation ring, working through next space created by the ch-4 loop of round 1; repeat from * around 3 times more, ch 5, join the round with a sl st in the first sc—5 ch-5 loops. Cut yarn leaving a 5-in. (12.7cm) tail. Fasten off. Weave in tail on the wrong side.

Step 6 For bottom layer, join color B with a sl st in any ch-5 loop of Step 5, in same ch-5 loop work (sc, hdc, dc, 4 tr, dc, hdc, sc), *in next ch-5 loop work (sc, hdc, dc, 4 tr, dc, hdc, sc); repeat from * around 3 times more, join the round with a sl st in first sc (5 petals made). Cut yarn leaving a 5-in. (12.7cm) tail. Fasten off. Weave in tail on the wrong side.

Step 7 Block the flower, as described below, taking care to block the petals of each layer separately.

Blocking the flowers
Step 1 Weave in all remaining loose tails on wrong side.

Step 2 Place flower on blocking surface. Working one petal at a time, carefully stretch petal into shape and pin edges. Space pins no closer than ⅛ in. (3mm) and no further than ½ in. (13mm). Pin each petal until entire flower is pinned.

Step 3 Pin all remaining flowers to blocking surface, spacing them about 1 in. (2.5cm) apart.

Step 4 Use spray bottle filled with warm water to lightly mist each flower until slightly moist. Do not soak flowers.

Step 5 Allow flowers to dry thoroughly, and remove pins.

On the block

You can use a well-padded ironing board or pad as a blocking board.

If flowers are not your thing, you can find patterns for a great variety of crocheted motifs for your headband in crochet books.

Sewing the flowers to the headband
Step 1 Arrange the flowers on the headband, and pin.

Step 2 Use a needle with thread to match each flower. Working from wrong side of headband, tack each flower to headband.

Danish Blooms Bag

Just because your bag is functional doesn't mean it has to be boring. I love the graphic, modern interpretations of botanicals that often find their way into Scandinavian designs. These designs always look beautiful against a rich wool fabric. Remember, this design is not about perfect circles but rather the beauty in the shapes of flowers.

Materials

Scraps of wool felt in shades of blue and green
Scraps of cotton prints
Fabric scissors
Straight pins
½ yd. (.46m) 10-in. wide (25.4cm)
   tear-away stabilizer
Sewing machine
Matching or contrasting sewing thread as desired
Fabric adhesive
Solid-color tote bag in wool

Blooming marvelous
For a different look, use a more traditional floral design, but be sure the shapes are simple and stylized.

If you prefer, stitch the flowers using satin stitch in a contrasting rather than a matching thread color.

Step 1 Each flower is made of three circles. You will need three circles in each size. From contrasting shades of felt, cut 4-in. dia. (10.2cm) and 2-in. dia. (5.1cm) circles. From print fabric cut, 3-in. dia (7.6cm) circles. The circles needn't be perfect; that's part of the charm of this design.

Step 2 Cut three straight stems and six leaves from green felt using the photograph as a guide.

Step 3 Cut two vines with leaves from green felt. Cut vines a little shorter than length of bag straps. For a more floral look, you may want to design your own flowers, leaves, and wavy vines.

Step 4 For each flower, pin large circle to a slightly larger piece of stabilizer. Machine-sew around circle using satin stitch or buttonhole stitch. Center medium circle on large circle, and sew in the same way. Repeat for small circle. Tear away stabilizer from assembled flowers.

Step 5 If desired, pin each leaf, stem, and vine to a piece of stabilizer, and machine-sew around as in step 4. Tear away stabilizer.

Step 6 Use fabric adhesive to glue felt pieces to bag.

Pearl Button Purse

For a subtle take on evening sparkle, pearl buttons are a nice change from the usual sequins. I buy jars of buttons at flea markets so that I have lots of them lying around for a project such as this. If you want speedy results, you could decorate this bag without taking out the lining, but a new lining will make it even more special.

Materials

Fabric clutch purse

Embroidery scissors

Large selection of pearl buttons in assorted shapes
     and sizes

Hand-sewing needle

Sewing thread in light pink, or as desired,
     to sew buttons

Seam ripper

⅓ yd. (.30m) cotton print for lining

Straight pins

Fabric scissors

Sewing machine

Sewing thread to match lining

Pearly whites

If the vintage pearl buttons you purchase are grimy, give them a wash before using them. Put a tiny amount of liquid soap in a jar with warm water. Put in the buttons, and shake the jar to agitate them. If there is any stubborn dirt left, use a soft brush to scrub it away.

Step 1 Cut lining from purse using embroidery scissors. Do this neatly, leaving a ½-in. border (13mm) of lining attached to bag. Set lining aside.

Step 2 Using shape of purse as a guide, arrange buttons in an attractive design on your work surface. I've arranged mine in a random pattern, clustering buttons at the frame and then spacing them gradually farther apart toward bottom of purse.

Step 3 Have a doubled-strand of thread in needle. Begin and end sewing on inside of purse. For each button, begin with knotted thread and end by knotting thread on inside. Start sewing at frame, slightly overlapping buttons as in photograph.

Step 4 Use seam ripper to separate lining removed in step 1 into two pieces. Use one piece as pattern. Fold lining fabric in half, matching short edges. Pin lining piece to fabric. Cut out, adding 1 in. (2.5cm) to top edge. Machine-stitch side and bottom seams same as original lining. Fold top edge ½ in. (13mm) to wrong side, and finger press. Place lining in purse. Pin folded edge to border of original lining, about ¼ in. (6mm) from frame. Hand-sew lining to border using slipstitch. (See "Slipstitch" on page 20.)

Quick Shoe Embellishments

Shoes may seem like they would be difficult to embellish, but a quick trip to the trimming store proves otherwise. You can adorn all your shoes with pretty trims, charms, or beads, customizing them to reflect your many stylish whims. I personally like the designs on my shoes to face me (otherwise it just looks weird when I look down at my feet) but it's really up to you. Here are a few ideas.

Materials

²⁄₃ yd. (.61m) ⁷⁄₈-in. wide (23mm) velvet ribbon in green
Fabric scissors
Ruler
Hand-sewing needle
Matching thread
Jewelry adhesive
2½-in. long (6.4cm) oval cameos
Pair of gold leather flats

Baroque shoe trims

Step 1 Cut ribbon into two 12-in. lengths (30.5cm). Thread needle, and knot end. For each ribbon, sew running stitches ⅛ in. (3mm) from one long edge. Gather ribbon to about half its length. Turn ends under and form into an oval. Test-fit cameo on oval, and either tighten or loosen gathers. Knot thread to hold gathers. (See "Running stitch" on page 20 and "Ruffles" on page 29.)

Step 2 Protect work surface from glue drips. Fold ends of gathered ribbon to wrong side and glue.

Step 3 Apply jewelry adhesive to gathered edge of ribbon, keeping the oval shape. Glue cameo to center of ribbon oval. Be careful not to get excess glue on ribbon.

Step 4 Determine which way you want cameos to face. They can either face you or face the world. Referring to photograph, glue ribbon oval to shoe.

Materials

Jewelry adhesive

1 yd. (91.4cm) ½-in. wide (13mm) red, white, and blue jacquard ribbon

Fabric scissors

⅔ yd. (61cm) ⅜-in. wide (10mm) blue-and-white ribbon

Ruler

2 1-in. dia. (2.5cm) buttons

Pair of red fabric flats

Preppy shoe trims

Step 1 Protect work surface from glue drips. For each shoe, begin at back of shoe, and use jewelry adhesive to glue red, white, and blue ribbon around edge of shoe. Trim end to allow for 1-in. overlap (2.5cm) with beginning of ribbon. Fold under end ½ in. (13mm). Glue into fold, and glue end to shoe.

Step 2 Cut blue and white ribbon into four 6-in. lengths (15.2cm). Mark center of wrong side of ribbon length with glue. Fold both ends to glued center and adhere. Repeat for remaining three ribbon lengths.

Step 3 For each shoe, glue together two ribbon pieces to make a bow. Glue bows to top center of shoe. Glue button to center of bow. Do not get excess glue in button holes.

Materials

¹⁄₃ yd. (.30m) 1¹⁄₂-in. wide (3.8cm) red-plaid ribbon
¹⁄₃ yd. (.30m) ⁷⁄₈-in. wide (23mm) blue-plaid ribbon
Fabric scissors
Straight pins
Hand-sewing needle
Matching sewing thread
Jewelry adhesive
Two kilt pins in gold
Size 12 beading needle
Beading thread in white or transparent
Twenty-four 6mm pearls
Pair of yellow canvas flats

Punky shoe trims

Step 1 Cut each length of ribbon in half. Trim ribbons so that they are unequal lengths. Cut ribbon ends into dovetails as shown.

Step 2 Fold each ribbon roughly in half. Fan ends out, layer blue plaid on red plaid; and pin close to fold. Hand-sew ribbons together; close to fold.

Step 3 Protect work surface from glue drips. Apply jewelry adhesive along non-opening edge of kilt pin. Refer to photograph. Clasp of one kilt pin should face left and other face right. Fold sewn edge of ribbon assembly over glue to secure. Let dry.

Step 4 For one shoe. Thread beading needle, and double-knot end. Add dot of glue to knot. String on five pearls. With clasp of kilt pin facing left, align fourth pearl on ribbon fold, to left of ribbon edge. Insert needle into ribbon fold, and exit at left of fourth pearl. Pull thread tight. Pass needle back through fourth and fifth pearls. Make small stitches at back of ribbon fold to secure. First three pearls strung at left will hang free.

Step 5 String three pearls on needle. Skip last pearl strung, and pass needle through second and first pearl. Make a stitch into ribbon fold, and pull thread tight. Make small stitches at back of ribbon fold to secure.

Step 6 String four pearls on needle. Skip last pearl strung, and pass needle through third, second, and first pearl. Make a stitch into ribbon fold, and pull thread tight. Make small stitches, and knot at back of ribbon fold to secure. Trim thread close to knot. Dot knot with glue.

Step 7 Open kilt pins, and secure to top of shoes, making sure clasps face away from each other.

Step 8 For other shoe. follow steps 4 – 6, changing "left" to "right."

Quick step

Sometimes I have extra scraps left over from projects that would be perfect for shoe embellishments. Studs, flat-back jewels, and buttons would work wonders on simple flats or heels.

Bias tape is also a great embellishment for shoes. Apply the bias tape by gluing the shoe edge inside double-fold bias tape. Bias tape works well with shoes because it goes around curves with ease.

Ultraviolet Scarf

Duplicate stitching mimics the look of intarsia knitting, but the technique is actually based on embroidery. For this project, I was inspired by the colorful screen-printed flowers of Andy Warhol, and so I named the scarf after one of his Factory regulars.

Materials

Graph paper (optional)
Pencil
Highlighter
Scarf knitted in stockinette stitch
3 colors of yarn in same weight and yarn in scarf
Size 16 tapestry needle
Embroidery scissors

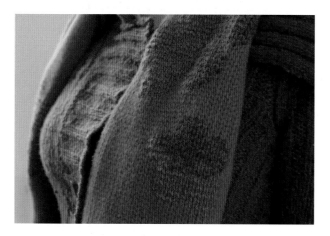

Step 1 In the chart on page 172, each square represents one duplicate stitch. This design has three flowers on one end of scarf, and one flower on other end. You can alter size of flowers, if needed, by making your own chart on graph paper. (See "Duplicate stitch on knits" on page 37.)

Step 2 Thread needle with yarn, and knot end. A duplicate stitch is an embroidered V-shaped stitch covering a V-shaped stitch on knitted item. Bring needle from wrong side of knit to right side at bottom of a V. Insert needle into top right end of V, and exit at top left end of V. Insert needle back into bottom of same V to complete stitch. To end a strand of yarn, make a few tiny stitches on the back. Cut yarn close to stitches.

Step 3 Follow chart to embroider design. Cross off completed rows using pencil or highlighter so you won't lose your place in the chart.

Pattern tip

It's easy to create your own duplicate stitch chart using is graph paper and a pencil. Each square on the graph equals one duplicate stitch.

Home Furnishings

Don't limit yourself to clothing and accessories when embellishing. You might be surprised to find a wealth of furnishings crying out for a little embellishing around your home. Recycle vintage fabrics, add embroidery to plain napkins to make them suitable for a special dinner party, or brighten up your kitchen with painted tea towels.

Lord and Lady Pillowcases

These felt pillowcases are sure to make you and your loved one feel like royalty. When wool felt is washed it gets denser and softer, so don't forget to prewash the felt beforehand. Thereafter, I recommend dry cleaning the pillowcases to prevent further shrinkage.

Materials

Black fine-tip permanent marker

Fusible webbing

Paper scissors

13 in. x 17 in (33cm x 43.2cm) rectangles wool felt in brown and light pink

11 in. x 13 in. (27.9cm x 33cm) rectangles wool felt in turquoise and hot pink

Fabric scissors

Two pillowcases

Iron

Sewing machine

Matching sewing thread

Color mix

Before you begin, it's important to preshrink each felt piece in warm water. Wash each color separately. Blot off excess water and place them in a dryer. The felt will shrink in both length and width by 3 in.–5 in. (7.6cm–12.7cm).

Dry cleaning is recommended to ensure your pillowcases remain as beautiful as when you first made them.

Step 1 Enlarge patterns on page 171 to desired size. Use marker to trace motifs onto paper side of fusible webbing.

Step 2 Cut out motifs leaving 1-in. (2.5cm) border on all sides. Following manufacturer's directions, fuse webbing to wrong side of felt. Cut out appliqués. (See "Appliqué" on page 56.)

Step 3 Peel paper backing from oval appliqués and arrange on pillowcases. Press with iron for 10–15 seconds.

Step 4 Peel paper backing from silhouette appliqués and arrange on oval appliqués. Press with iron for 10–15 seconds.

Step 5 Use straight stitch and matching thread to machine-sew around oval and silhouette appliqués.

Trompe l'oeil Lampshade

Chandeliers are the ultimate in design sophistication, but are often pricey and a big hassle to install in a rental apartment. This modern and easy-to-make lampshade would look stunning hanging from the ceiling over a single light bulb or on a large floor lamp. The chandelier images appear to be complex stencils, but they are really image transfers printed on an ink-jet printer.

Materials

Color ink-jet copier/scanner/printer
Four to five sheets iron-on image transfer paper
(Note: quantity depends upon size of lampshade.)
Paper scissors
Iron
¼ yd. (.23m) cotton fabric in white
Fabric scissors
Newspaper
Spray adhesive
13-in. dia. (33cm), or larger, drum lampshade in white
Embroidery floss in desired colors
Size 7 embroidery/crewel needle
Embroidery scissors
20 chandelier drops in crystal or acrylic
Satin-finish spray paint in desired color
Tape measure
Awl
Needle-nose pliers
Twenty 8mm jump rings in gold

Lights out

For more elaborate embellishment, embroider on the image transfer after transferring it to the fabric and before adhering it to the shade. Use the decorative embroidery stitches shown on pages 31 and 32, working them in floss colors that reflect the décor of your room.

Step 1 Scan chandeliers on page 170, enlarging as desired. (See "Image transfers" on page 61.)

Step 2 Following manufacturer's directions, print four to five chandelier images onto image transfer sheets.

Step 3 Cut out, leaving ½-in. border (13mm) on all sides.

Step 8 Adhere chandelier images to lampshade, in desired position, referring to photographs.

Step 9 Thread needle with three strands of embroidery floss and knot end.

Step 10 Use running stitch to sew chandelier images to lampshade. (See "Running stitch" on page 20.)

Step 11 In well-ventilated area (outside if possible), place chandelier drops on newspaper, and apply an even coat of spray paint. Allow to dry, turn over, and spray other side.

Step 12 Measure circumference of bottom of shade. For a 13-in. dia. (33cm) shade, the circumference is slightly more than 40$^{13}/_{16}$ in. (1.0m). For spacing of chandelier drops, divide the circumference by 20. For this size lampshade, spacing is slightly less than 2$^1/_{16}$ in. (5.2cm). Use awl to lightly pierce shade 20 times just above bottom wire. The holes are for jump rings, so keep them small.

Step 13 For each crystal drop, use needle-nose pliers to open a jump ring. Slip drop onto jump ring. Insert one end of open jump ring into hole in shade. Use pliers to close jump ring.

Step 4 Place fabric right side up on smooth, hard surface (not an ironing board). Position transfer, face side down. Following manufacturer's directions, iron the transfer.

Step 5 When transfer is cooled, peel off transfer paper carefully. Check that image has been completely transferred. If it hasn't, go over area again with iron.

Step 6 Cut around chandelier images, leaving ½ in. (13mm) border of fabric on all sides.

Step 7 Place chandelier images, face down, on newspaper, and apply spray adhesive.

Folk Art Tea Towels

Some people may think potato-printing is for children, but the process is perfect for creating graphic Scandinavian-style designs. I also love the idea that I can run to the corner store to pick up my printmaking supplies. Make sure to buy yourself a big bag of potatoes to experiment with because potato printing is addictive.

Materials

Tracing paper

Pencil

Chalk-backed dressmaker's paper

Lightweight cardboard

Paper scissors

Potatoes

Sharp knife

Paper towel

Fine-tip permanent marker in black

Lino cutting tools

Cotton or linen tea towels

Fabric ink in two different shades of orange, yellow, turquoise, and green

½ in. (13mm) sponge brush

Ruler

Iron

Making a stamp

Step 1 Trace motifs on pages 170 and 171. Use dressmaker's paper to transfer motif onto cardboard. Cut out template. (See "Transferring with chalk-backed dressmaker's paper" on page 30.)

Step 2 Cut potatoes in half lengthwise using knife. Blot excess moisture with paper towel. (See "Potato printing" on page 59.)

Step 3 Use marker to trace template onto cut side of a potato.

Step 4 Use lino cutting tools to cut around outline of template, then remove all areas that should not print. Lino cutting tools are very sharp so always cut away from yourself. Put finished stamp in refrigerator for an hour before printing.

Stamping a motif and heat setting

Step 1 Place towel on work surface. Brush fabric ink onto stamp. Use even pressure to stamp onto towel.

Step 2 Allow ink to dry thoroughly. Heat-set with iron following manufacturer's directions.

Seed pod tea towel

Step 1 Cut one large and one small seed-pod stamp.

Step 2 Use two different orange inks to stamp pods in both sizes all over towel.

Flower-stalk tea towel

Step 1 Cut stamps for flower center, petal, stalk, and leaf.

Step 2 Use yellow ink, and stamp flower center in center of towel width and about 2 in. (5.1cm) from end of towel.

Step 3 Stamp a turquoise petal on either side of flower center as in photograph.

Step 5 Stamp green stalks down center of towel.

Step 6 Stamp green leaves next to stalks as shown.

You say potato...

You can use your potato stamps again. They will keep in the refrigerator for a day or so, but after that, throw them away, and start again.

Use potato stamps to print on all kinds of surfaces, including paper, fabric, canvas, and even walls.

If you want to print one color over another, allow the first color to dry completely, or the colors may run together. This could be an interesting effect, but experiment on scrap fabric first.

For best results, make sure the ink is applied evenly to the stamp. This will ensure nice, sharp prints. Reapply color as soon as the print begins to break up.

Woodland Creatures Etched Glasses

I love the subtle texture created by etching glass. It's more modern than glass painting and it goes with everything. Plus, it's an easy, inexpensive way to update simple glassware. As with all chemicals, work in a well-ventilated area, wear protective gloves, and cover your work area and clothing. Because it takes a little practice, you might want to try out the technique first on a glass jar or bottle. I experimented with empty tomato-sauce jars before I moved on to glassware.

Materials

Glassware (Note: Straight-sided round glasses work best. If glass has squared sides, etch only on flat areas.)
Fine-tip permanent marker in black
Translucent self-stick vinyl
Paper scissors
Craft knife
Lint-free cloth
Rubbing alcohol
Cotton swabs
Protective gloves
Etching cream
1-in. wide (2.5cm) sponge brush

CAUTION
Etching cream is a chemical. Wear protective eyewear and gloves, and work in a well-ventilated space.

Finger tips
Cleaning fingerprints from the design areas with rubbing alcohol before you apply the etching cream is vital! Be careful to hold the glass on the vinyl-covered areas, and don't touch the areas to be etched.

Step 1 Clean glassware thoroughly. (See "Etching" on page 65.)

Step 2 Enlarge stencil patterns on page 173 to desired size.

Step 3 Cut a piece of translucent self-stick vinyl slightly larger than stencil. Slip stencil under vinyl, and trace using marker.

Step 4 Use cloth and rubbing alcohol to clean stencil area of glass. Do not touch this area with your fingers once it has been cleaned. Peel off backing paper, and apply vinyl to glass.

Step 5 Use very sharp craft knife to cut out stencil. Remove vinyl from stencil area. Cover your finger with clean cloth, and firmly smooth cut edges of design to glass.

Step 6 Check stencil area for finger prints. Use a cotton swab and rubbing alcohol to wipe them away. Don't allow alcohol to touch edges of stencil. It will dissolve the vinyl's adhesive.

Step 7 Following manufacturer's directions, brush a thin layer of etching cream on stencil area.

Step 8 Wait specified amount of time, then rinse glass under running water, and peel off vinyl. When glass is dry, etched design will be visible.

Etched stripes

You make etched-glass designs without using a stencil. Use strips of clear or translucent tape to outline stripes or other straight-sided motifs such as squares, polygons, etc. Etch as you would for a stencil. The tape will rinse off in hot water.

Framed Inspiration Board and Button Pushpins

Forget those generic corkboards. To get your creative juices flowing, you are going to need a really beautiful inspiration board. I use mine to tack up postcards, tear sheets from magazines, old photos, and anything else that inspires creativity. Adorable button pushpins make the board even more fun to use.

Materials

For the inspiration board:

Picture frame in desired size

Medium- and fine-grit sandpapers

Tack cloth

Acrylic paint in desired color

1-in. wide (2.5cm) paintbrush

Water-based varnish

$^3/_{16}$-in. thick (5mm) foam board cut to fit frame

Print fabric cut 2 in. (5.1cm) larger on all sides
than foam board

Hot-glue gun

Glue sticks

Twelve 1$^1/_4$ in. (32mm) wire brads

Tack hammer

Ruler

Pencil

Awl or ice pick

Two 1$^1/_2$-in. long (3.8cm) sawtooth hangers with nails

For the button pushpins:

Pushpins

Assorted buttons

Heavy-duty wire cutter (optional)

Jewelry adhesive

Mix it up

Another design option for button pushpins is to layer buttons and glue them together before adhering to the pushpin. Adding a small brass charm to the top button is a nice touch.

Don't feel that you have to use identical buttons for your pushpins. Using a variety of sizes, colors, and designs will make your board even more exciting and different.

Step 1 Sand frame, first with medium-grit sandpaper and then with fine-grit sandpaper. Wipe sanding dust off using tack cloth.

Step 2 Paint frame following manufacturer's directions. Apply two to three coats, as needed. Allow each coat to dry for two hours.

Step 3 Apply two coats of varnish. Allow each coat to dry for two hours.

Step 4 Place fabric, right side down, on work surface. Center foam board on fabric.

Step 5 Apply line of hot glue on one long edge, 1 in. (2.5cm) from edge and both corners. Immediately fold fabric over edge of foam board, and smooth it onto hot glue. Repeat for other long edge, this time pulling fabric so it is smooth and tight on front of foam board. Hot glue is hot, so be careful to protect your fingers.

Step 6 Repeat step 5 for short edges of foam board.

Step 7 At each corner, fold fabric neatly, and adhere with hot glue.

Step 8 Place covered board in frame. Use wire brads hammered into back of frame to secure board. Use at least three wire brads on each side.

Step 9 On back of frame, measure and mark 2¾ in. (7.0cm) from each corner of frame top.

Step 10 Measure and mark ¾ in. (19mm) from top of frame to each mark made in step 9.

Step 11 Position each sawtooth hanger centered on mark made in step 9. Place top edge of hanger at mark made in step 10.

Step 12 Use awl to make pilot holes for nails. Secure hangers with nails.

Making the button pushpins
Step 1 If there is a sewing shank at back of button, clip it off using wire cutters.

Step 2 Apply small amount of jewelry adhesive to top of pushpin and back of button. Adhere pushpin to button, and allow to dry.

Collector's Napkins

I love to look at beautifully displayed collections of natural objects. These napkins were inspired by display cases filled with exotic insects. Due to the nature of embroidery, each insect will look a little different, and each of your collector's napkins will be one-of-a kind. These napkins would be a special wedding gift for a couple too cool for monograms!

Materials

Chalk-backed dressmaker's paper
Cotton or linen dinner napkins
Straight pins
Pencil
Embroidery hoop
Embroidery floss in colors as desired
Size 7 embroidery/crewel needle
Embroidery scissors
Terrycloth towel
Iron

Bugs, bugs, bugs

Not a fan of bugs? Look through copyright-free books published by Dover Publications for inspiration.

These designs would look great on clothing or fabric accessories. I like the idea of them on crisp pillowcases.

You can also draw your own designs, and transfer them onto the napkins.

Step 1 Enlarge motifs on page 173 to desired size.

Step 2 Place photocopy over napkin and slip dressmaker's paper, chalk side down, under photocopy. Pin both to fabric to prevent shifting while you work.

Step 3 Working on a hard surface, go over all lines using a sharp, hard pencil. Check image by lifting up a corner of photocopy and dressmaker's paper. (See "Transferring with chalk-backed dressmaker's paper" on page 30.)

Step 4 Place transferred area of design on napkin in embroidery hoop. (See "Embroidery" on page 30.)

Step 5 Thread needle with three strands of floss for all stitches. To begin and end a strand of floss, make tiny stitches on wrong side of napkin.

Step 6 Use backstitch for details and outlines. Fill larger areas with satin stitch. Other decorative stitches can be used as desired. See stitch illustrations on pages 30 to 32.

Step 7 Place embroidery, right side down, on folded terrycloth towel, and iron to remove wrinkles.

Woolen Bunny

This little bunny is inspired by my very own real-life muse, Potato. I started making little bunnies out of sweater scraps to give to my friends shortly after my husband and I adopted Potato. He spends days with me in my craft room "helping" me sort fabric, chewing on my papers, and hopping all over my projects. I couldn't live without him.

Materials

Lightweight cardboard

Chalk-backed dressmaker's paper

Pencil

Paper scissors

Water-soluble pen

Felted sweater (for bunny body)

Assortment of felted sweater scraps (for details)

Straight pins

Fabric scissors

Size 7 embroidery/crewel needle

Embroidery floss in desired colors

Embroidery scissors

Two buttons, matching or in different colors
    as desired

Sewing machine

Sewing thread to match

Fiberfill stuffing

Chopstick or other pointed tool

Hand-sewing needle

Step 1 Enlarge bunny on page 172 to desired size. Use dressmaker's paper to transfer bunny onto cardboard. Cut out template. (See "Transferring with chalk-backed dressmaker's paper" on page 30.)

Step 2 Pin template to sweater. Use water-soluble pen to trace template onto wrong side of sweater. Cut out bunny from both thicknesses. Cut out details from felted scraps, and pin to right side of bunny.

Step 3 Use three strands of floss in needle, and knot end. Sew details to bunny using whipstitch. Embroider nose using backstitch and satin stitch. (See photograph of whipstitch on page 23 and "Embroidery" on page 30.)

Step 4 Sew on buttons for eyes. If the bunny is a gift for a child, sew an "x" for each.

Step 5 With right sides facing, pin front to back. Use straight stitch to machine-sew ½ in. (13mm) from edge. Leave 3 in. (7.6cm) opening in one side.

Step 6 Clip corners and curves. Turn right side out, using chopstick to push out ears, arms, and legs.

Step 7 Pull off small pieces of stuffing, and push them tightly into bunny using chopstick. Stuff ears, arms and legs first.

Step 8 Turn edges of opening to inside, and pin opening closed. Hand-sew opening using slipstitch. (See "Tips" on page 21 and "Slipstitch" on page 20.)

Tulips and Tweed Jacket, page 99

Garden Vine Shrug, page 96

Folk Art Tea Towels, page 157

Folk Art Tea Towels, page 157

Vivienne Vest, page 108

Mod Squad Tee,
page 74

Center

Daisy Sundress, page 110

Lord and Lady Pillowcases, page 152

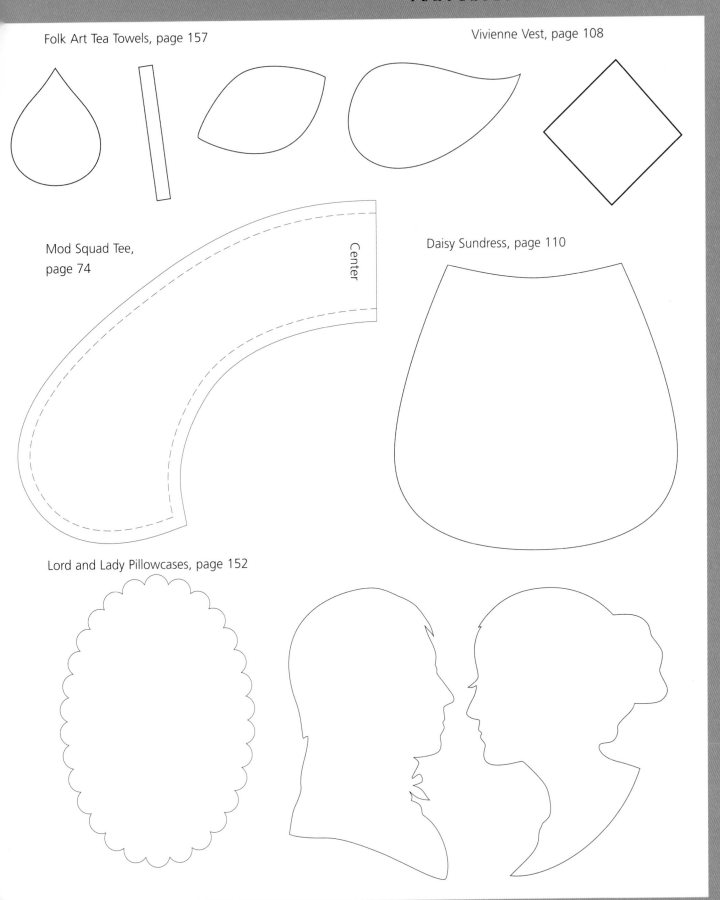

Little Bird Mini, page 116

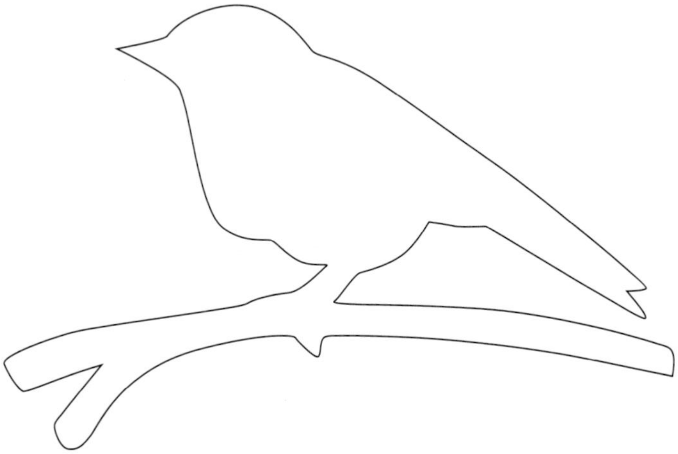

Woolen Bunny, page 168

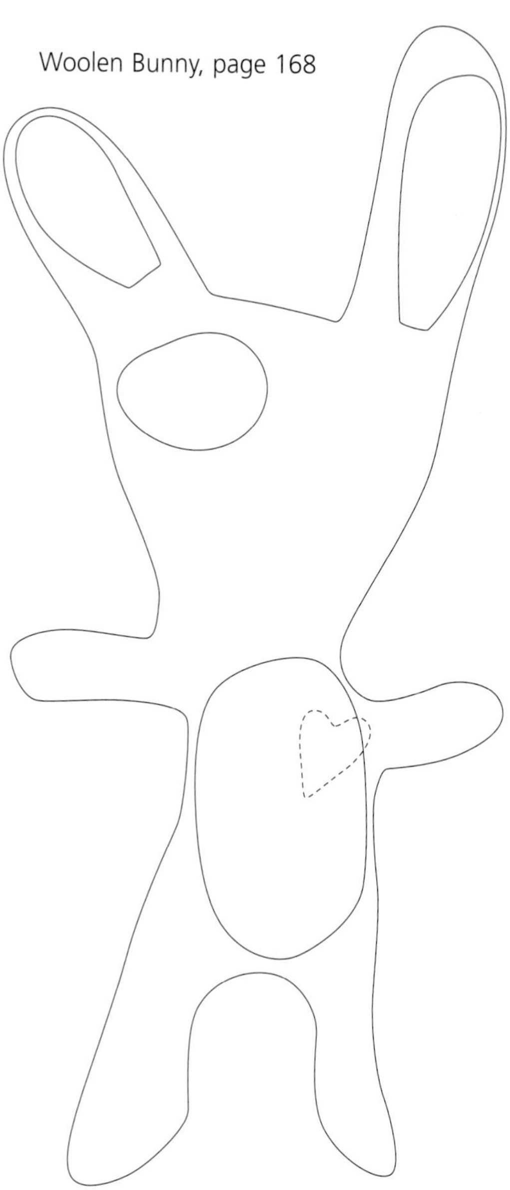

Rainy Day Skirt, page 94

Ultraviolet Scarf, page 148

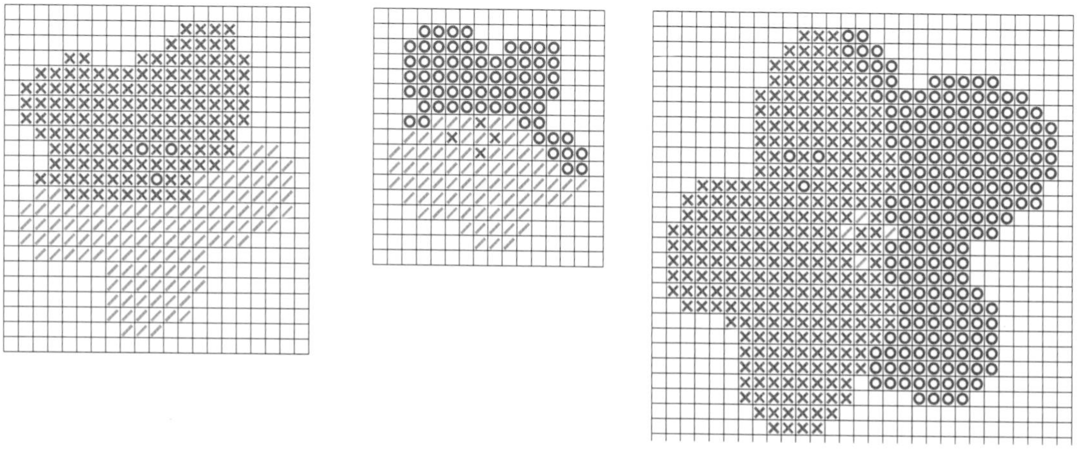

Woodland Creatures
Etched Glass, page 160

Collector's Napkins,
page 166

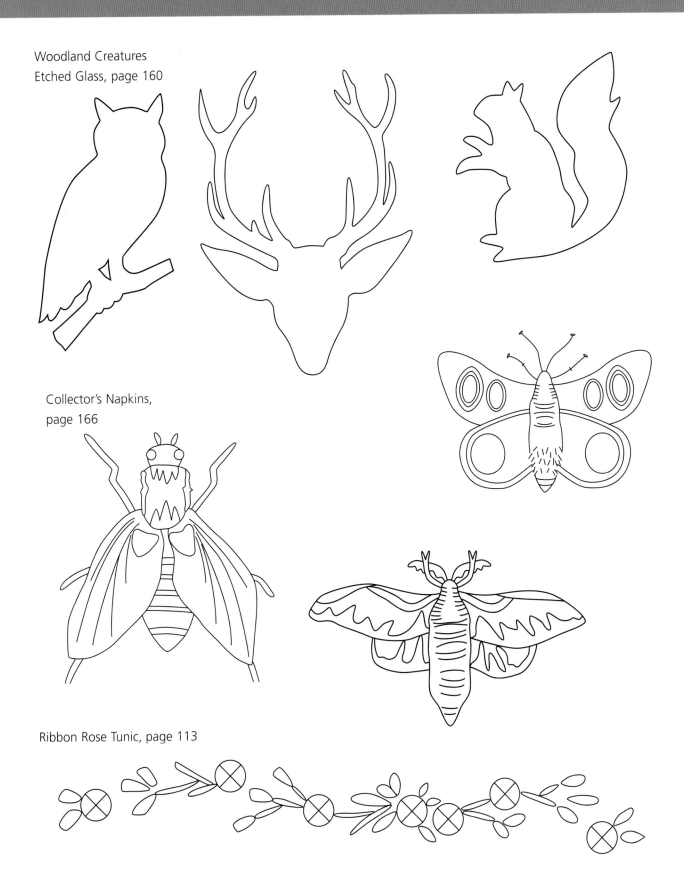

Ribbon Rose Tunic, page 113

Deco Sweater,
page 106

Trompe L'oeil Lampshade,
page 154

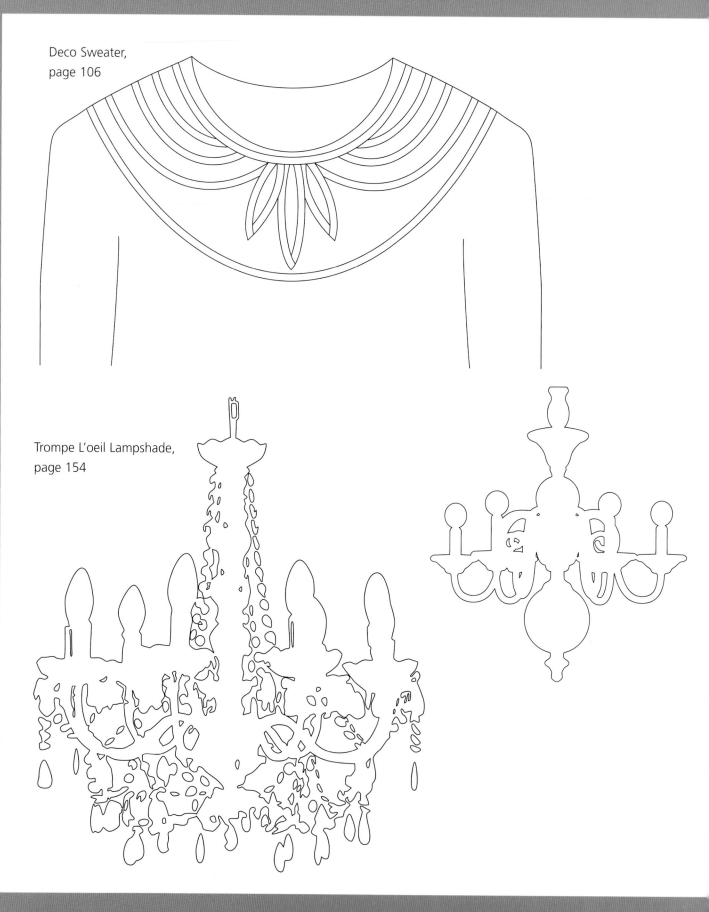

Index

Resources

Ambatalia Fabrics
1 El Paseo
Mill Valley, CA 94941
Tel: 415-388-6278
Web site: www.ambataliafabrics.com
Green, organic, rare, and vintage fabrics

Anthropologie
85 Fifth Avenue
New York, NY 10003
Tel: 212-343-7070
Web site: www.anthropologie.com
Clothing, jewelry, and home accessories

Dharma Trading
1604 4th Street
San Rafael, CA 94901
Tel: 800-542-5227
Web site: www.dharmatrading.com
Dyes, resists, and fabric paints

Dover Publications
31 East 2nd Street
Mineola, NY 11501
Tel: 800-223-3130
Web site: www.doverpublications.com
Transfers, templates, patterns, and art

Metalliferous
34 West 46th Street
New York, NY 10036
Tel: 212-944-0909
Web site: www.metalliferous.com
Metal, findings, and beads supplies

Purl
Purl Patchwork
147 Sullivan Street
New York, NY
Tel: 212-420-8798
Web site: www.purlsoho.com
Fabrics and materials

Prairie Point Junction
124 East 8th
PO Box 184
Cozad, Nebraska 69130
Tel: 308-784-2010
Web site: www.prairiepointjunction.com
Quilt and cotton fabrics, patterns, and wool felt

The City Quilter
133 West 25th
New York, NY
Tel: 212-807-0390
Web site: www.cityquilter.com
Quilting fabrics, books, and tools

Reprodepot Fabric
www.reprodepot.com

Superbuzzy
www.superbuzzy.com

Etsy
www.etsy.com

Sew Mama Sew
www.sewmamasew.com

Acknowledgments

I would like to thank so many people for making my first book possible.

My wonderful editors, Michelle, Katie, and Marie for taking a chance on this first-time author, letting me be myself at all times and showing me a great time in London! My agent, Lauren, for keeping me organized and sane. I'm not sure how I could have done this without you, and honestly, I'd rather not think about it.

An amazing creative team: Michael and Mark for making the projects come alive with wonderful photography; Gemma for creative vision; Ella for "getting my aesthetic" and making the models look fierce! Christina for recommending me to Michelle—without you, this book wouldn't exist! Anne for helping me "make the pretty;" and Kim for her skilled hands and crochet expertise. All the Department of Craft folks for being crafty gods and goddesses. My crafty gal-pals near and far: Courtney, Daisy, Jenn C., Jenn S., Kari, Linda, Lorelei, Margaret, Meredith, Sarah G., Sarah O'C., Sherri, Susan, and all the other glitter girls and crafty bloggers out there. I couldn't imagine better friends and inspirations.

My family, especially my four parents, Patty and Steve and Michael and Tricia, and my little brother, Jesse, for always being supportive and never questioning why I would want to play with fabric for a living. A big extra thanks to my mom, Patty, who spent one crazy fall weekend helping me make things, and who has been my crafty super-hero since day one. And one giant thanks to Adam, my partner in life and craft. Thank you for your encouragement, love, and patience. You are amazing.